BIRDING AT POINT PELEE

D1598641

BIRDING AT POINT PELEE

A BIRDER'S HISTORY OF ONE OF CANADA'S MOST FAMOUS BIRDING SPOTS

HENRIETTA T. O'NEILL

JAMES LORIMER & COMPANY LTD., PUBLISHERS
TORONTO

James Lorimer & Company Ltd. acknowledges the support of the Ontario
Arts Council. We acknowledge the support of the Government of Canada
through the Book Publishing Industry Development Program (BPIDP) for
our publishing activities. We acknowledge the support of the Canada Council
for the Arts for our publishing program.We acknowledge the support of the
Government of Ontario through the Ontario Media Development
Corporation's Ontario Book Initiative.

Cover design: Meghan Collins

Library and Archives Canada Cataloguing in Publication

O'Neill, Henrietta

The Canada Council | Le Conseil des Arts
for the Arts | du Canada

Birding at Point Pelee / Henrietta O'Neill.

Includes bibliographical references.
ISBN-13: 978-1-55028-933-6
ISBN-10: 1-55028-933-0
1. Bird watching—Ontario—Point Pelee National Park—History. I. Title.
QL685.5.P64O53 2006   598.072'3471331   C2006-903620-9

James Lorimer & Company Ltd.,Publishers
317 Adelaide Street West, Suite 1002
Toronto, Ontario, M5V 1P9
www.lorimer.ca

Printed and bound in Canada.

Photo credits:
Al Collison: 139; Jim Flynn: 113, 158, 171, 208; Don MacDonald: 70
Henrietta O'Neill: 186; Point Pelee National Park: 14, 32, 45, 56, 98, 100,
154, 197; Steve Pike: 168, 176; Susan Ross: 212; Sikkema Family: 204;
Robert R. Taylor: 24, 79, 97, 122, 163, 214; Alan Wormington: 118, 132

Illustrations:
William A. Martin: 11, 19, 30, 50, 63, 88, 106, 128, 161, 179, 202; Robert R.
Taylor: 73; George M. Stirrett & Nora Mansfield: 183

Contents

"We never go to Point Pelee without something interesting happening."

-Percy A. Taverner, 1906

Preface

I sit before my computer, the last chapter on my screen. It has been a long time. I know some of the stories weren't told and some of the interesting people didn't get mentioned. I wish I could have included them all.

I remember my introduction to this culture. A "rude awakening" might be a better way to describe it. It was 6 a.m. one morning in May 1995, and there were people with binoculars everywhere. I had just been driving the Point Pelee National Park shuttle for a few weeks and still couldn't believe that visitors would actually get up in time to catch the first trip to the Tip. I had heard of birders coming to Point Pelee but I had never witnessed anything like this. People filled both wagons of the shuttle as soon as it stopped at the Visitor Centre.

As I worked, I found it easy to get caught up in the excitement of the day. I enjoyed listening to the stories of the older birders. They were slower, more relaxed, and always willing to tell a good tale. They talked about driving to the Tip, camping on the beach, parking wherever they had a mind to, and bird banding. I hated to think that all this history would vanish into obscurity with them. "Someone should write this down, write a book, otherwise it will all be lost!" I said to one elderly gentleman. "Why don't you do it?" he replied.

Several years have passed since that day. The book is complete. I trust that your history has been well cared for in my hands. I return it to you for your enjoyment, for your appraisal, and for your continued safekeeping.

Acknowledgements

I owe a debt of gratitude to those birders, too numerous to mention individually, who got me interested in their culture and activity. They suggested I "do the writing," contributed stories of their own, and encouraged me throughout the project.

I owe much to Robert R. Taylor, who conducted interviews with many of the "old timers" for me. He encouraged me throughout the project and added valuable insight into the Point Pelee bird-banding era. He also donated pictures and answered my technical questions about reproducing them.

My thanks go out to William A. Martin, who was my "sounding board," allowing me to float ideas and giving me much needed, and appreciated, feedback. Along with James Woodford, Gilda Swartz, and Tom Hince, he also read various chapters and drafts. The finished product is better because of the work put in by these people.

I would not have been able to write this book without the assistance of Glenn Coady, who helped me gain access to some much needed material from the Toronto area.

My thanks also go to Alan Wormington, who gave me access to his extensive library. His knowledge of Point Pelee and of birding in general was a source of valuable information. He meticulously reviewed the manuscript and his comments greatly enhanced the final version.

Various family members were behind-the-scenes helpers. They read through early drafts, helped me with their computer skills, and wondered when I would finally crawl out from under my piles of paper, turn off the computer, and give them some attention.

To the reader who does me the honour of picking up this book and reading it, I hope that it is all that you expected, and more.

CHAPTER 1

Point Pelee: A Migration Highway Through Carolinian Canada

William Hosea Ballou stood just outside the tree line that September day in 1877, and allowed his gaze to follow the shore of the gently curving sandspit. He stooped to examine a few small birds that had been weakened by storms and lay exhausted on the beach. As he did so, a shadow passed between him and the early morning sun. Looking up, he saw not one, but several Sharp-shinned Hawks ranging overhead in search of prey. He watched in amusement as several hawks descended upon a flock of sandpipers. The sandpipers dove into the water out of harm's way only to resurface some distance from shore.

To the other members of the landing party, who were mapping topography and hydrography between Point Pelee and the Detroit River, the swarms of hawks trolling above them held little significance. To twenty-year-old William Ballou, however, these birds were worth noting.

From where Ballou stood on the sandbar at the Tip of Point Pelee facing north, he could look to his right and follow the long sweep of shore reaching back and curving east. Along this side of the outstretched point, and enclosed by a slight ridge of sand, there lay acres upon acres of marsh. Some areas were dry enough to wade through while others

deepened into ponds of considerable size. For early survey-
ors such as himself, the east side of Point Pelee was a
quagmire and a constant threat of illness, but for hunters of
waterfowl it was both a source of income and of food. Ballou
noted the tremendous crop of Wild Rice growing in the
marshes that fall, and he predicted that the enormous flocks
of blackbirds occupying the area would remain all winter.[1]

Looking to his left, Ballou could see beach stretching
northwest in a twenty-four-kilometre-long curve toward
Leamington. The sandy ridge along this side was higher,
broader, and much more stable. A mixed forest, largely of
Eastern Red Cedar and Black Walnut, grew along the ridge.
Small groves of White Pine stood out here and there, while
close to the Tip there was a heavy growth of Eastern Red
Cedar interspersed with Ground Juniper. Ballou knew from
experience that there was a narrow, rutted road just inland
that ran parallel to the west side of Point Pelee. A small
mixed farming community was nestled between it and the
marsh edge. The whole of Point Pelee formed a triangle. Its
northern base was approximately five-and-a-half kilometres
wide, while the converging sides of the triangle were four-
teen-and-a-half kilometres long. This triangle, on the apex
of which Ballou stood, stretched out into Lake Erie in such
a way as to encourage diurnal migrants following the shoreline to gather at its tip. What Ballou saw that September,
and later described, was an annual migration occurrence.

William Hosea Ballou, born September 30, 1857 at
Hannibal, Oswego County, New York, was an amateur
naturalist. In the summer of 1877 he was working as a
recorder for a lake survey being conducted by the United
States government. The task was to map the topography as
well as the inshore and offshore hydrography of Lake Erie.

The surveying team was led by Lieutenant Colonel C. B. Comstock, Corps of Engineers, United States Army, who described their progress in various reports. He stated that in 1875, the party, after making a survey of the Niagara River, began one of Lake Erie. By the end of the season they had followed "the north shore to a point 5 miles [eight kilometres] west of Port Colborne ... [In 1876] the hydrography and topography were completed about Long Point."[2] In a submission to the House of Representatives, Comstock reported: "On May 8 and 10, 1877, the triangulation parties of Assistant Engineers Wisner and Woodward, the shore parties of Assistant Engineers Lamson, Towar, and Terry, and the steamer Ada, commanded by Lieutenant D. W. Lockwood, were sent into the field, and are now continuing the work westward from where it closed last fall."[3]

As part of the on-land survey team, Ballou spent time on the south shore of Lake Erie, on several islands, on Maumee Bay and River and Detroit River, and on the north shore of Lake Erie. He made natural history observations which later appeared in print. In 1878 his article titled, "The History of the Islands of Lake Erie," was published in *Field and Forest*, a monthly bulletin for the Potomac Field Naturalists' Club. Ballou described his findings on the islands and listed birds nesting there, including Black-billed and Yellow-billed Cuckoos, Bald Eagle, Virginia Rail, Spotted Sandpiper and, on Pelee Island only, Common Loon. He described Black Water Snakes, "darting through the water, sneaking out from under every foot-step, sunning themselves in heaps, knots and snarls on the tops of low bushes, stray logs, and rocks,"[4] and speculated that not many birds would nest on the islands because there were so many snakes. He also described his theory that the Detroit and Maumee Rivers, coming into

The gateway into Point Pelee National Park as seen in the 1950s

Lake Erie almost exactly opposite each other, created the chain of islands and shoals between Point Pelee and Sandusky. Ballou believed that the western edge of Lake Erie was much farther east at one time.

Ballou was the first to speculate on paper about the role Point Pelee plays in bird migration. In the September 1877 issue of the *Oologist*, a magazine aimed at collectors of birds' eggs, Ballou theorized that this wedge-shaped tract of land and marsh, jutting out into Lake Erie, served as a funnel for migrating land birds. He believed that they followed the shore to the end of the Point, where they would gather in preparation for their advance across the lake. Once they made it to the Tip of Point Pelee, migrating birds were within a short flight of Pelee Island, then Middle Island, Kelleys Island, and finally the Ohio mainland. It was Ballou's thought that Point Pelee and the islands formed a natural causeway for travelling birds. In his writings, he noted Merlin and Sharp-shinned Hawks in swarms, attacking the migratory birds as they stopped to rest, thus securing easy and abundant prey. He wrote that he could not recall a "single instance of noticing a specimen on the whole range of lake coast on the southern shore, from Toledo to Ogdensberg, or on the Canada shore east of Point aux Pelée."[5] Ballou did not consider that this might be a migration route for hawks as well, rather, he connected the numbers of hawks solely to the abundance of food due to the migrating passerines.

After his work on the survey during the summer and fall of 1877, his continuing education began at Northwestern University in Evanston, Illinois. Ballou then went on to the University of Pennsylvania, where he studied natural science, obtained an honors ScD at Fort Worth University, and finally law degrees from the Chicago Law School and the College of Oskaloosa, Iowa.[6]

William Hosea Ballou would not become a renowned figure in the natural history of Point Pelee, but it was he who put the Point Pelee migration phenomenon on the map with his early observations. His reports eventually set off a trickle, then an avalanche, of visiting birders, that Ballou working in the sun that September day, could never have envisioned.

Carolinian Canada

Dr. William Brodie dozed off to the sound of the train wheels clicking on the rails. He was heading home to Toronto after spending a few days studying Point Pelee in July 1879. Brodie had taken the stage from Windsor to Leamington, where he made his headquarters, and from which he made frequent excursions into the surrounding district. He had slogged through swamp, stumbled over rough pasture, plodded up one sand dune after another, just to half run, half slide down each, with underbrush slapping his face and catching his clothes on the way. He fought his way through tangles of grape, bittersweet, and Virginia Creeper, then trekked miles of Point Pelee's sandy shoreline. The heat and humidity of the summer added to his fatigue.

In spite of the conditions he must have encountered, Brodie persisted, making daily trips around Point Pelee. In the process, he spoke to numerous local residents who claimed to have seen a "visitation of war birds." He was intrigued; from the physical description of this "all red" bird, he believed that these were male Northern Cardinals.[7] The influence of Lake Erie on Point Pelee weather allowed for an extended frost-free growing period, attracting—by 1832—the first European farmers. The DeLaurier, Abbott, Mooney, Bickford, Girardin, LaFleur, and Edwards families were squatters who were already agitating to get clear title to their land on Point Pelee. Brodie wondered if this same mild weather might not be attracting the cardinal to extend its range into Canada. There is no indication that Brodie ever actually saw a cardinal during his visit.

What he did find, however, was Northern Waterthrush. These birds were fall migrants, making themselves at home in the marginal area between cleared farmland and marsh. Some local schoolchildren gave Brodie a specimen of Yellow-breasted Chat: the bird had flown in through an open window of the school and had been killed hitting the glass in an opposite window. To Brodie, the presence of this particular bird was a clear indication of a warmer climate. If he needed further proof, he had only to look at the thriving plant community. Swamp Rose-Mallow was over seven feet tall and Prickly Pear Cactus was "common, growing in clumps on dry sandy situations."[8]

Dr. William Brodie was in his late forties at the time of his visit to Point Pelee. Born in Aberdeen, Scotland, he immigrated with his parents and grew up on a farm in the County of York, Canada. He taught school, working his way through to become one of the first graduates of the Dental College in Toronto. He started his own, very successful, dental practice. An avid reader and naturalist, Brodie founded the Toronto Entomological Society in 1877. His own particular fascination was galls, the hard, round, growths on plant stems, and the insects they contained. His fascination was so great that on one occasion, while showing his collection to a fellow enthusiast, he summarily dispatched a patient who had come seeking relief from a toothache to another dentist. In 1903 he gave up dentistry and took charge of the Biological Department of the Provincial Museum. As provincial biologist, Brodie had a great deal of influence on young naturalists and was considered the heart and soul of natural history in Toronto.[9]

Although he was not known to have visited Point Pelee again, it is undoubtedly with Brodie's encouragement that other naturalists did. It is also his letter to a fellow naturalist that documented the second most important aspect of Point Pelee—its southern nature. Not only is this the southernmost part of mainland Canada, but its climate is also moderated by the waters of the shallow western basin of Lake Erie. Pelee's warm, humid weather, its excellent marsh habitat, and its gently curving shoreline are all part of the unique ecosystem of southern plant and animal associations that

Brodie found. Yellow-breasted Chat, Northern Cardinal,
Blue-gray Gnatcatcher, Carolina Wren, and Bewick's Wren
are just some examples of more southern bird species discovered by the first wave of ornithologists to study Point Pelee.
Visiting botanists such as Alfred Brooker Klugh noted the
presence of Black Walnut, Eastern Red Cedar, Northern
Hackberry and Tuliptree. Dr. William W. Newcomb
collected several Olive Hairstreak Butterflies, a species for
which he had been unsuccessfully searching in the Detroit
area. Zebra Swallowtail, Spicebush Swallowtail, Giant
Swallowtail, Tawny Emperor, Hackberry Butterfly, and
migrating Monarch butterflies were seen and documented.
In short, at Point Pelee one could see and collect southern
flora and fauna found almost nowhere else in Canada.

Chapter 2
Exploration

A Great Horned Owl hooted as two friends prepared to bed down for the night in a small wooded area near Point Pelee's eastern beach and just south of today's Hillman Marsh. Overhead, in silhouette against a silver moon, small land birds flew. Thirty-nine-year-old William Edwin Saunders, and travelling companion Harry Gould, tried to relax that evening, but anticipation made for fitful sleep. The date was September 19, 1900. Rising early to a meagre breakfast, they gathered their gear and made their way east along the rutted country road. Here they saw Dickcissels arguing over a patch of remnant weeds, while unidentified flocks of ducks winged past far to the south. Northern Harriers circled overhead in search of small and unwary rodents. Upon reaching East Beach, Saunders and Gould turned south, their destination the end of the Point. They noted Black-bellied, Semipalmated, and Golden Plover, along with Killdeer, Sanderling, and Baird's Sandpiper. Herring, Ring-billed, and Bonaparte's Gulls were seen loafing in large numbers on old pound-net stakes protruding from the water just offshore, while Common and Black Terns skimmed past, sometimes almost close enough to touch.

The naturalists stopped halfway down East Beach to eat a simple lunch of bread and butter. As they did so, the wind picked up, blowing sand against their faces and dropping it into the pot of lake water boiling for tea. They wasted little time for the sandy beach made walking slow, and their aim was to make it to the end of the Point by nightfall. As planned, the Eastern Red Cedars there sheltered them for the night.

Working their way north along the west side of Point Pelee the following morning, dense evergreen and deciduous habitat led Saunders and Gould to expect different species of birds than they had encountered the previous day. They were not disappointed. They saw a Black-and-white Warbler creeping along a dead branch, investigating crannies in the bark for bugs, while Black-throated Blue, Black-throated Green, Bay-breasted, Chestnut-sided, and Blackpoll Warblers flitted lightly amongst the late summer foliage. A few Golden-crowned and Ruby-crowned Kinglets hid in the conifers, popping out from amongst the branches and disappearing as fast, all the while chittering in agitation. Gray-cheeked and Swainson's Thrush moved quietly through the underbrush as Cooper's and Sharp-shinned Hawks trolled overhead for unwary prey: clusters of feathers on the leafy forest floor displayed their success.[10]

This trip to Point Pelee in September 1900 was not the first taken by William Edwin Saunders. W.E. Saunders was a pharmacist from London, Ontario, who had been a student of natural history since childhood. His father, Dr. William Saunders, also a pharmacist, was an entomologist who encouraged all of his sons in their scientific pursuits. It was not surprising then that W.E.'s first trip to Point Pelee should be in the company of one of his brothers. They spent almost three weeks in August and September 1882, and were most impressed by the Passenger Pigeons that flew back and forth along the length of the Point. The experience encouraged W.E. to return to continue his investigation of Point Pelee and its birds.

In June 1884, accompanied by his brother Arthur P. Saunders, and Mr. William L. Bailey of Philadelphia, W.E. scoured the Point. On June 1 they found Dickcissels in every suitable habitat. In a meadow about two miles from the end of the Point, after a great deal of searching, and then only because W.E. flushed a female off her nest, they were able to collect a nest and five eggs—the first Canadian nest record for Dickcissel. On June 6 a Yellow-breasted Chat was heard, and two days later a female was finally found and collected. Connecticut Warblers were "quite common at Point Pelee, for a few days in June, as ground feeders in dry places, where several were procured."[11] Northern Bobwhite "were not very common although they were found nearly to the end of the Point at least as far as the cultivated lands reached."[12] Near the west side of one of the ponds, W.E. found a Common Loon's nest and understood from local residents that they were known to breed there annually.[13] (By 1905, Common Loons were only being seen as regular migrants.) W.E. became acquainted with the hunters and farmers living on the Point, creating a network that would serve him well during his frequent trips from London with various friends.

One such friend was James Edward Keays, who was known to the Saunders family through his four-year apprenticeship in pharmaceuticals with W.E. Saunders & Company. It was Keays who learned from the locals at Point Pelee about the existence of Northern Cardinals in the area when he, along with his cousin H.H. Keays, visited in September of 1901. They confirmed Brodie's initial belief that the Northern Cardinal was extending its range into Canada, via Point Pelee, by collecting a young male. Keays also noted only one Northern Bobwhite on the Point, although the hunters reported it to have been plentiful at one time. His record of a Hairy Woodpecker, a scarce bird at Point Pelee, was significant, as was the change he noted from just two Yellow-bellied Sapsuckers observed on September 18 to a hundred on September 21, and a flight of four hundred Northern Flickers that same day.[14] With these records, Keays added to the growing evidence of the importance of Point Pelee as a migration site.

In May 1905 W.E. Saunders invited two young birders from the Michigan Ornithological Club to meet him in Leamington for their first experience at Point Pelee: Percy A. Taverner, a Canadian architectural draftsman living in Michigan, and Bradshaw Hall Swales, a lawyer and ornithologist. Of that trip Taverner said:

> It is a difficult place to reach from here. We had to get up, catch two street cars and a ferry, pass customs and catch a 6:15 a.m. train that put us in Leamington about 7:30. There we waited for Saunders' train at 8:49. He came all right and on time, and we took a rig that was to drive us to the east base of the point. ... As we left Leamington we passed through a very slightly hilly country, the most noticeable features being the stumps of peach orchards killed the winter before last. Stray red cedars showed here and there and the fences were full of White-crowned Sparrows.[15]

Upon hearing the calls of a Yellow-breasted Chat, they stopped the horse and went chasing, with the result that W.E. acquired one chat and Taverner shot a Whip-poor-will. They continued to the east shore and, after sending the buggy back to Leamington, began the long walk south to the tip of the Point. Taverner was astonished by the differences between the east and west sides of Point Pelee. The east side consisted of one relatively bare sand dune, while the west was lined with thickets of Eastern Red Cedar and juniper that bordered a road running parallel to the shore. On the inland side of the road, there were farm houses and fields "supporting a thrifty-looking farming community ... This is in striking contrast to the [east side of the Point] where there was but one building to be seen the whole way."[16] As they walked south on the eastern beach, they found Piping Plover, Dunlin, Least Sandpiper and a male Hudsonian Godwit. Common, Caspian, and one Black Tern were also seen. The three collected specimens as they travelled; when they camped for the evening in a Red Cedar grove on the west side of the Point, they went to sleep to the sound of a Whip-poor-will's plaintive call. The following day they woke to the sight of warblers everywhere, including a fleeting view of a Connecticut. Both Baltimore and Orchard Orioles were a common sight. Although rain had dogged them for the better part of this trip, it is easy to imagine their exultation as they headed back to Leamington on foot. Taverner and Swales now understood W.E.'s enthusiasm: Point Pelee was an excellent place for bird study. They planned a second visit during fall migration and resolved to return as often as possible.

Accordingly, Taverner returned September 4, 1905 with Alfred Brooker Klugh, an instructor at the agricultural

Spring warblers

college in Guelph. They set up camp in the same area as on the previous visit and Taverner dubbed it "Camp Coues," in honour of Elliot Coues, author of the first guide to North American birds. Klugh's main interest was botany and he "discovered a treasure with every step."[17] On one excursion into the bushes, Klugh returned with the rare catch of that visit, a Connecticut Warbler. Throughout the first couple of days, Taverner marvelled at the continuous stream of warblers migrating down the west side of the Point: "Never saw birds so thick in my life over such an expanse of territory. Usually in the fall the warblers cruise about in companies but here on the point the whole place seems to be occupied by one large company."[18] By the time Swales joined them on September 7, the warblers were all but gone except at the extreme tip of the Point, "as though they were leftovers that had reached the jumping off place."[19] This wave-like movement recorded by Taverner would become a familiar pattern to birders visiting Point Pelee in the future.

While Taverner, Swales, and Klugh studied bird movement on the Point, another ornithologist was spending time on the Lake Erie islands to the south. Dr. Lynds Jones, associate professor of zoology at Oberlin College, Ohio, had evidence supporting the theory that birds turned west toward the islands after flying south out of sight of observers on Point Pelee. Jones, who designed and taught the first college course in ornithology in 1895,[20] was studying the islands as well as the southern shore of Lake Erie and had acquired some data of his own. He insisted that he had seen birds "coming to the easternmost point of Pelee Island from nearly due east."[21] This supported the theory advanced by Ballou in 1877 that diurnal migrants used the islands as stepping stones. However, Taverner and Swales claimed, "As far as we could discern their forms with our glasses they followed a straight and undeviating course that would land them on the Ohio shore some four or five miles [six to eight kilometres] to the east of the city of Sandusky."[22] The argument was not heated; the ornithologists were simply trying to unravel the secrets of migration from their different perspectives. Jones advanced evidence of immature birds of some species migrating ahead of adults—including Brown-headed Cowbird, Red-winged Blackbird, orioles, and warblers. Taverner concluded that in other species, such as shorebirds, adult birds migrate first. Taverner also noted: "Here as every individual has to pass through a limited space where nearly all can be noted and none pass through unobserved the very earliest will be noted and the very beginning of migration can be detected."[23] Both naturalists discuss the need for simultaneous, co-operative work by competent observers over a wide area. Unfortunately this did not happen, although, between the naturalists at Point Pelee and Lynds Jones on the Lake Erie islands, a great deal was being discovered.

Meanwhile, Taverner's enthusiasm for Point Pelee as an excellent location for ornithological research continued to build. His friend and confidant James Henry Fleming, a businessman, ornithologist, and collector from Toronto, Ontario, made his first appearance at Point Pelee on May 19, 1906. Fleming, a protege of Dr. William Brodie who, after the death of Fleming's father, became his mentor and friend, was also acquainted with W.E. Saunders. Joined by Swales, Saunders, and Taverner on this trip, Fleming managed to secure a Chuck-will's-widow—the first Canadian record—and a Northern Mockingbird, while Swales and Taverner worked to collect Carolina Wrens. Taverner described the event as follows:

> This was about nine o'clock of the 20th in the red cedar along the road near the end of the Point ... It [the Chuck-will's-widow] flushed at the feet of Swales and settled again in full sight immediately. It obligingly waited for me to get out of the line of shot when Fleming secured it ... It proved to be a male ... There are no records for this species anywhere about in Southern Ont. ... On the return trip, about opposite Grubb's fish house on the East shore, Fleming distinguished himself by taking a Mockingbird. Fleming says this is the first authentic record for Ontario.[24]

The increasing number of unusual records brought another phenomenon to light—that rarities and vagrants show up at Point Pelee with some regularity—which would serve to increase the place's reputation as a birder's paradise.

The mere presence of rarities was interesting, but W.E. wanted to know more about the rare breeding birds of the area and he resolved to determine the parameters of their nesting range. On June 6, 1909, with James Stirton Wallace, a Toronto businessman and naturalist, as a travelling companion, W.E. set out on an amazing walk along the shore of Lake Erie from Amherstburg to Blenheim: a distance of at least ninety-four kilometres as the crow flies. Species on which they wanted to focus were Northern Cardinal, Carolina Wren, Bewick's Wren, and Yellow-breasted Chat. Their first interesting discovery was several pairs of Piping Plover nesting at the mouth of "a big creek a few miles from the Detroit River."[25] Although W.E. was aware of the fact that they also nested on the Point, he knew that breeding grounds for Piping Plover were rare on the north shore of Lake Erie, so this was a happy find. He noted that they recorded as many as ten Grasshopper Sparrows a day, that chats, cardinals, and Carolina Wrens were all found in many locations, and that two Dickcissel males were found singing in a field near Blenheim. The latter were especially noteworthy as, after being quite common in southwestern Ontario, W.E. had not encountered a single one in the previous five years. The acquisition of the first specimen of Acadian Flycatcher in Canada was the most celebrated occurrence of this excursion "and brought the trip to a very successful close,"[26] in Blenheim on June 10.

A number of other significant birds were recorded during these years of exploration. Two Tufted Titmice were found by Wallace near the end of the Point—one of which W.E. collected—on May 2, 1914. This was the first Canadian record for this species.[27] A Bewick's Wren taken April 3, 1917, was important given the context that there were as many as five of these wrens heard or seen that day, establishing the likelihood that it was a regular resident of Ontario.[28] A Bachman's Sparrow—another new record for Canada—

was taken by Prof. J.W. Crow and W.E. on April 16, 1917, and became specimen number 4,140 in W.E.'s collection.[29] Two more species added to Point Pelee's list were a Louisiana Waterthrush, which W.E. found April 23, 1920, and an Alder Flycatcher, caught August 17, 1923, by W.E. and F.A. Saunders. W.E. remarked that it seemed strange after nineteen years of work to collect such a common bird as the Alder Flycatcher as a new species on the Point.[30]

As the ornithologists studied and collected birds at Point Pelee, they also recorded other kinds of natural phenomena such as erosion, inclement weather, and biting insects. One fall Taverner and Swales planned to stay at Point Pelee for several days, but Stable Flies made working an impossibility. Taverner recorded his frustration with the whole situation: "The worst plague however and what almost spoiled the trip and did cut it short by a couple of days was the number of flies. They were ten times as bad as last fall and there was no keeping them out. We had netting over the tent door but in spite of this they came in in droves."[31] The naturalists avoided mosquitoes, another irritation, by bedding down on the sweet smelling new-mown hay in a farmer's hayloft. Taverner exulted in the fact that "though great gaping cracks opened in the walls all around us, there was not a single mosquito there."[32]

During periods of inclement weather the ornithologists observed birds forced out of natural habitats. One such event took place May 1908, when an unseasonably cold spring with snow and heavy gales put a great deal of Point Pelee under water. The marsh was flooded, causing "Gallinules and Coots to paddle around in broad daylight while Bitterns, both American and Least, unable to reach the muddy bottom ... were congregated along the steep shores ... and ... could be watched with ease." Other marsh birds were driven well into the bush; rails and Marsh Wrens foraged under Eastern Red Cedars. Whip-poor-wills were found in the middle of clearings and among "mullein stalks toward the end of the Point."[33] Flooding caused by heavy rain in the first week of May was a problem the following year. That spring the migrating birds were late. But even so, Wallace collected a Summer Tanager in a grape arbour near the tip of the Point, the third specimen for Ontario,[34] and added it to Taverner's collection. Taverner noted a change in the length of the sandspit at the end of the Point. Between a visit made April 23 and another the first weekend in May, 275 metres of the tip had disappeared and "a short spit reaching only about 20 yards [18 metres] south east had been formed."[35]

The naturalists first observed erosion on East Beach and the Tip in 1906. Investigating the phenomenon, Taverner found residents of Point Pelee who had long been concerned about it. Their claim that "thirty years ago one could almost walk dry-shod to within a quarter of a mile [about four hundred metres] of the old dummy lighthouse that is now just visible from the end of the point"[36] brought Taverner to believe as they did that at least some of the damage was being done by offshore sand dredging. Consequently, in 1915, when Taverner had the opportunity to make a report to the Commission of Conservation in Ottawa, the problem of erosion at Point Pelee was included in his discussion.

CHAPTER 3

The Great Lakes Ornithological Club

Members of the Great Lakes Ornithological Club (GLOC) relaxed in front of their clubhouse at Point Pelee. By October 3, 1909, the club had already reached its zenith and soon the members would be busy elsewhere, but the picture taken that day remains, as does the information that these men gathered during their visits to the Point.

Sitting on the steps, legs crossed, hands clasped around his knee, is James Henry Fleming. Fleming had a passion for collecting. More than a birdwatcher or an active collector, Fleming bought and sold specimens and skins from all around the world. He was actively involved in both North American and European ornithological organizations, making him a powerful friend to have in the birding world.

Percy Algernon Taverner, who sits perched above Fleming on a board running along the top of the fence in the picture, was inclined to be impulsive. A dreamer and a romantic, his writing was lyrical in its descriptions rather than systematic and austere. This artistic side of Taverner irritated Fleming, who saw it as a drawback to serious scientific endeavour.

On the fence beside Taverner sits William Edwin Saunders (W.E.). W.E. was the oldest of the group: a leader and a teacher (in the broad sense of the word). He was the facilitator of the group, and the one who recommended Point Pelee as the place for study.

Standing beside W.E. is Bradshaw Hall Swales, Taverner's young and ambitious American birding companion. In 1889, at the age of fourteen, Swales had his first article published in the *Oologist*. By the time he was twenty-one, he had a list of thirty-four titles to his credit in various magazines of the day.[37]

James Stirton Wallace, who stands at the end of the group, was really its heart. He had no great aspirations to ornithological glory and was willing to devote some of his time to the drudgery of camp life. He was friendly, helpful, and likeable.

"The Shack," as this little building was affectionately christened, was their clubhouse on Point Pelee, and the men called themselves The Great Lakes Ornithological Club.

In 1905, when the club was formed, natural history clubs were abundant, and these men were involved in clubs in their own communities already. Why then did they feel the need to start an organization of their own, one that would involve travelling distances that others might see as a deterrent? Taverner and Swales belonged to the Michigan Ornithological Club, but they were unimpressed by the degree of scientific understanding and type of activity indulged in by their fellow members there. Taverner called them "egg collectors" and bemoaned the fact that they kept few notes.[38] Taverner was working on a hypothesis concerning the movement of some migrating birds.[39] Fleming was studying irruptions of Thick-billed Murre, the results of which he was to present to the Fourth International Ornithological Congress in England, in June of 1905.[40] Both were having problems acquiring much-

The Great Lakes Ornithological Club members relax in front of the shack at Point Pelee, 1909.

needed data, and agreed that a bird survey of the Great Lakes was long overdue. Taverner suggested starting a club to do this research. There were interested and competent people available; the problem was the distance separating them. Could a club work under such circumstances?

With Swales and Taverner in Detroit, Klugh in Guelph, and Fleming in Toronto, it must have seemed propitious that W.E. Saunders lived in London—a fairly central location. Keays (also from London), Swales, Taverner, Klugh, and Fleming, were invited to spend the last weekend of February 1905 with W.E. in order to discuss the formation of a club. They planned to keep the club exclusive, and since they wanted to focus their studies on the birds of the Great Lakes, it was grandly dubbed the Great Lakes Ornithological Club.[41] Fleming had been unable to make it to London for the initial meeting but was nevertheless considered a founding member.

At the first meeting, the club was given its name, an expedition to Point Pelee was planned for May, W.E. became secretary, and Klugh was asked to draw up a constitution. The constitution, which consisted of seven clauses, was included in the first club bulletin going out to the membership March 22. With the exception of the clause concerning the bulletin, all were agreed upon by the members.

It was initially proposed that since the members lived at a distance from one another, they would keep in touch and share information by means of a circulating bulletin. Any member who wished to make a contribution to the bulletin would send it to W.E., who, when he had enough material, would begin the circulation by sending it to the first member on the list. Each member could add his comments and eventually the bulletin would return to W.E., who would send it, along with all the added comments, and new material, back to the first person on the list. As the bulletin went around for the second time, each contributor was expected to send his article along with any comments added to it by other members back to W.E., who would keep it on record. Fleming felt that, as the material would be preliminary, it was better for the authors to have the option of removing their own articles if they wished. Early in 1906 he presented an amendment to the constitution to that effect. W.E. preferred to receive the bulletins intact so that they would be available to the membership at a later date upon request. Taverner agreed with Fleming, suggesting that informality would encourage the members to contribute without fear of having the written words come back to haunt them. By the time this clause is being discussed, Dr. Lynds Jones (who had agreed to co-operate with Taverner and Swales by letting them know what he was finding while studying diurnal movements of birds on the islands and north shore of Lake Erie in September 1905) had accepted an invitation to join the club.[42] Jones, who had long been involved in ornithology and had been a founding member of the Agassiz Association in Grinnell, Iowa, in 1886, understood the importance of a written history and sided with W.E., who again tried to convince the members to save the bulletin intact. W.E. Saunders, Keays and Jones voted to preserve the bulletins, while Taverner, Fleming, Swales, and Klugh, voted to allow members to remove their articles. Unfortunately, this decision resulted in the loss of many written contributions.[43] However, as Taverner had hoped, the fact that the bulletin was informal gave the members the opportunity to float their ideas, questions, and suggestions, learning from one another while brainstorming in a friendly environment.

Club meetings were also informal, consisting of collecting trips to Point Pelee. As already mentioned, W.E. first introduced Taverner and Swales to the Point in May 1905. In September of that year Klugh joined Taverner and Swales for an extended stay. On those two trips, "Camp Coues" was set up under some Red Cedars on the west side of the Point. This would be their home away from home until The Shack was built in 1908. Meanwhile, the unusual southern flora and fauna as well as the excellent opportunity to watch migration, were attractions that would induce the naturalists to return on a regular basis. These factors would also convince Taverner to begin working on an annotated list of the birds found on Point Pelee. He asked for co-operation from the other ornithologists and wrote to Brodie, who had become a corresponding member of the GLOC in 1906. Brodie's letter of reply briefly describes his

1879 visit to the Point:

> I saw but few of the birds we find generally
> distributed over Ontario such as Song
> Sparrows, Robins, Blue Birds, but I found two
> species which do not occur at Toronto ...
> Water Thrush ... were rather common along
> the margins of marshes and small streams near
> the lake. ... [And a] Yellow-breasted Chat spec-
> imen ... was brought to me by school children.
> ... About ? way down the point, warblers were
> common in dense clumps of Red Cedar.[44]

With Brodie's information in hand, Taverner continued
his compilation of birds, fully intending that the authorship
of the project would be strictly his. However, Swales had
other plans. He was willing to co-operate with Taverner by
letting him use his notes, but he also expected to co-author
the paper. Taverner was upset and wrote to Fleming for
advice concerning this weighty problem. Fleming smoothed
the feathers of both young men and Taverner reluctantly
agreed to Swales' terms. "The Birds of Point Pelee" would
carry both names.

Taverner had one more disappointment in store—the
article would be published in the *Wilson Bulletin*, bulletin of
the Wilson Ornithological Club, rather than the American
Ornithologists' Union's more prestigious publication, the
Auk. Nevertheless, after it appeared, "The Birds of Point
Pelee" was given a favourable review in the *Auk* by J. A.
Allen,[45] although Fleming responded by warning Taverner
about "writing like a Sunday special."[46]

Because of its length, "The Birds of Point Pelee," was

published in six installments, from June 1907 to September 1908.[47] In its introduction all the members of GLOC were acknowledged for their input:

> W.E. who first introduced us to Point Pelee ... Klugh ... to whom special credit must be given for all the botanical notes ... Lynds Jones ... who, stationed on the Islands, co-operated with us on the Point in early September, 1905. ... The residents of Point Pelee ... whose good will and kindness made our trips, if not possible, at least comfortable.[48]

Next came a description of the Point:

> Near the western end of Lake Erie, project-ing into those waters some nine miles [fourteen kilometres] or so, ... two long low sand-bars meeting at the apex ... the triangle so inclosed ... is swamp of varying degrees of wetness [deepening] into ponds ... The eastern shore ... being composed of but a single sand-dune, bare of vegetation except for a meager covering ... The western side ... is heavily wooded ... [with] Carolinian indications.[49]

Then migration was discussed, quoting Lynds Jones on the islands:

> I found the birds migrating practically every-where along the line of the islands, but the largest and best defined stream was across

> Pelee Island ... No birds were seen crossing
> the Lake except in a line with the islands.[50]

Jones's statement was qualified with their own findings
on the Point where some species were "seen crossing
directly over."[51]

Following a thorough background on all aspects of Point
Pelee, the accounts of 209 species of birds begin. Along with
the fact that the Least Bittern is a common summer resident,
Taverner mentions that the local name for it is "strike-fire."
The Sharp-shinned Hawk warrants a three-page description
of its migration: "over the treetops, a steady stream of them
was beating up and down the length of the Point." Ruby-
throated Hummingbirds are described as "pugnacious little
mites."

In the final installment, September 8, 1908, Taverner
added a supplementary list to cover new species found since
the article was written, and a summary of subsequent trips to
Point Pelee. In Taverner's conclusion, he discusses the
species that led to more questions and conjectures. He points
out that further study is needed, and he ends by saying, "if we
have only succeeded in calling the attention of some of the
ornithological public to what seems to us to be one of the
most promising fields of migrational and distributional investigation we shall feel that we have accomplished our end."[52]

Meanwhile, the GLOC continued to make trips to Point
Pelee. In 1907, the final member was added, James Stirton
Wallace, thus bringing the number up to nine. In 1908 the
club members agreed to share the cost of building a clubhouse.[53] Taverner drew up the plans for a simple building
approximately five by six metres, gable roofed without
veranda or "architectural effects," with screened windows on

all sides, and two doors. It would be a permanent structure in which they could work, relax, and store their gear. In a letter to Fleming dated September 2, 1908, Taverner wrote: "It will be built in the shade of a couple of large walnut trees and on Bert Gardner's ground and in the enclosure his house is in so it will be under his eye and protection when we are not there." The land they planned to build on was a small lot leased from Bert Girardin (spelled Gardiner or Gardner by the naturalists) for a period of five years. In a letter to Fleming dated September 10, 1908, Taverner complained that the bids had run up to $160.00; nevertheless, The Shack, as it came to be known, was built. Here the club members maintained a record book of all sightings and notes pertaining to each stay.

The location of The Shack makes it obvious that club members trusted Bert and his brother Max Girardin. These two, along with Wid Grubb, Wallace Tilden, and Langille, were local farmers and hunters who appear frequently in the writings of the GLOC members. Bert, a bachelor living with his mother, seems to have been the most active and colourful amateur naturalist native to Point Pelee. He enjoyed spending an evening in discussion with the visiting ornithologists, and in spite of having lost one arm to a hunting accident, he was still considered an excellent shot.

Although Bert knew the Point from tip to base and was eager to share his knowledge and skill, not everyone got along with him. With the approval of the Canadian government, Norman A. Wood, an American naturalist and researcher, spent a month at Point Pelee in the fall of 1909 studying fall migration and collecting specimens for the University of Michigan. During that time he stayed in Bert's home and, although in his overview of the trip Wood thanked the residents of Point Pelee for their specimens and data, it was obvious to Taverner, who had spent some days there at the same time, that not all had run smoothly. Taverner stated: "We have got on the good side of the boys there by systematically over paying them. Not always in cash but in other ways ... It was a course of wisdom and we have not only bought their services but their good will which is beyond price to us."[54] Looking back many years later, he attributes this favour to the way in which W.E. understood the residents and his ability to deal with any peculiarities: "However it is largely through Will's engaging personality and influence that we became persona grata on the Point and received the many great and small tokens of friendship from local inhabitants that made our continued presence there possible and pleasant."[55]

After those halcyon years from 1905 to 1909, the Great Lakes Ornithological Club gradually disintegrated. Dr. Brodie died in 1909, Klugh moved to Kingston in 1906, and Taverner became Head of Ornithology at the Victoria Memorial Museum (Ottawa) in 1911. Swales became a member of the governing board of the Zoological Museum at Ann Arbor beginning in 1912, and for a number of years was honorary assistant in ornithology there. In 1918 he joined the Smithsonian Institution and moved to Washington.[56] Fleming seldom visited Point Pelee, while Keays had been a less active member from the beginning.[57] W.E. Saunders and Wallace continued to bird at Point Pelee until Wallace died in an accident while pruning a tree at Fancy Free Island on Rideau Lake, July 24, 1922.[58] W.E. visited Point Pelee September 26, 1922, but he "spent most of the time roofing the shack and saw few birds." He found the visit difficult because the residents liked Wallace and he

had to "tell each group over again the story of his accident."
In his notes of that visit W.E. says of Wallace, "Jim had
visited the Point more often than any of the other members
and was usually the propelling influence that determined
our visits. He was always the one that took on himself the
responsibility and drudgery of the camp work."[59] The Shack
would remain open to members and their visitors until 1924
when Bert Girardin sold his house to the Richards family.
W.E. wrote a letter to Swales, Taverner, and Fleming letting
them know that Richards wanted to buy the shack for
$100.00. He felt that the club members should accept the
offer, and a later description by W.E. of a visit to the Point
on August 30, 1924, indicates that they took his suggestion:
"First visit since our shack was attached to [Richards']
house. ... Slept upstairs in Bert's house, and had too many
[Richards], well meaning but in the way."[60]

Although the Great Lakes Ornithological Club era had
come to an end, it was only the beginning of Point Pelee's
popularity, as club members continued to sing its praises
wherever they went. For W.E. Saunders, Point Pelee would
continue to be the place to bring birders and watch migration. His enthusiasm, personality, contacts through
involvement in various organizations, and writing and
speaking ability was unequaled. In the words of Taverner,
"At home he built up a following among the young and old
... he introduced many to new interests until London
became a center of many observers with him as the clearing
house and energizer ... he visited camps, schools, and nature
and social service clubs, lecturing."[61] Charles Maddeford,
who went on to lead the McIlwraith Ornithological Club
(named for Thomas McIlwraith, a well known and
respected naturalist from Hamilton, Ontario, who wrote

The Birds of Ontario in 1886) as president from 1934 to 1935,[62] gives much credit for his involvement to W.E. Saunders:

> My friend, Reg Werner and I met Dr. Saunders when we attended the McIlwraith club in 1922 as student members. He spoke so highly of Point Pelee that we determined to go there. He told us of Bert Gardiner and that we could probably stay with him. During the Easter holidays of 1922 we took the train and eventually arrived at Leamington. We had shipped our bicycles ... the roads were a sea of mud. Dr. Saunders had written ahead and we ... stayed with Mr. Gardiner for three days ... We were inexperienced bird watchers but we had a book and saw some birds never seen before or since at Pelee. ... Dr. Saunders had a very magnetic personality. He made everything so interesting and made them seem so important. He appealed particularly to students. Many went on to make it their life work. Bill Girling and Keith Reynolds were the most outstanding but there were many others.[63]

W.E. enjoyed encouraging young naturalists, but was in his glory when he could introduce Point Pelee to visiting ornithologists such as Dr. Joseph Grinnell, of the University of California at Berkeley and president of the American Ornithologists' Union (AOU). On October 23, 1931, the AOU was holding its annual convention in Detroit. The meeting included a field trip to Point Pelee, which W.E.

later described in the *London Free Press* this way:

> I had the pleasure of introducing Dr. Grinnell
> ... to the Point ... We had the great good luck
> to see a small flight of hawks and other inter-
> esting birds. ... during our stay at the tip of
> the point, we saw two of these little birds
> [Black-capped Chickadee] come down to the
> last trees and make a faint-hearted attempt at
> passing over to Ohio ... A still rarer bird was
> the White-breasted Nuthatch. ... I have
> reserved for last the single item that thrilled
> the Canadians and had a correspondingly
> depressing effect on the Americans, namely
> the migration of Starlings ... on this day at
> Point Pelee we saw flock after flock ... sail
> over the lake with much less hesitation than
> most birds evince, and while we watched
> them out of sight for Ohio, in the name of
> Canada we presented them with sarcastic
> words to our friends from the south. When
> they vehemently declared they neither
> needed nor wanted them we threatened to
> charge them an export duty on these birds.[64]

As one of seven elected members at the first meeting of
the American Ornithologists' Union in 1883, W.E. was well
known by the membership.

From an early age W.E. belonged to various nature clubs,
beginning with the Entomological Society into which he
paid his membership dues at the age of eleven, in February
1873. His first paper was published in the *Canadian*

Entomologist in 1879. He lobbied in favour of the Ornithological Section of the Entomological Society and became its first president in 1890. This organization exists today as McIlwraith Field Naturalists of London Ontario Incorporated. W.E. became a member of the Wilson Ornithological Club in 1902 and was its president 1912-13.[65] Then, while attending the founding convention of the Federation of Ontario Naturalists (FON) in 1931, he was unanimously elected president, and chaired its first public meeting, held February 26,1932.[66] W.E. described that meeting with some pride: "To that meeting came men from Kingston, Hamilton and London, who joined with the members in Toronto to make a meeting representative of the province."[67] The fact that the FON would regularly hold annual trips to Point Pelee is in itself a testament to W.E.'s influence, but the list of speakers to a 1937 regional gathering proves that other Point Pelee enthusiasts were involved as well. Wallace Tilden, a Point Pelee resident; Robert Grant, Superintendent of Point Pelee National Park; and Dr. George Stirrett, who was at that time secretary-treasurer of the Kent Nature Club, were all on the agenda.[68]

Stirrett was an excellent choice for a speaker as he was by that time well on his way to making the study of Point Pelee his life's work. He was a founder of the Kent Nature Club and involved in the formation of the FON. His interest in Point Pelee began when he moved to Chatham in 1926, while working for the Ministry of Agriculture.[69] He was appointed the first chief parks naturalist for the Canadian Parks Service in April 1959,[70] and in that capacity implemented many excellent ideas to facilitate interpretation for all Canadian National Parks. Among the improvements planned at Point Pelee by Stirrett were the Woodland

Nature Trail and Marsh Boardwalk. When Stirrett moved
to Kingston, he began the Kingston Nature Club, and after
joining Parks Canada and moving to Ottawa, he became
active in The Ottawa Field-Naturalists' Club. All the while,
Stirrett wrote natural history articles for local newspapers
under the pen name "Graham Vail."

For W.E. Saunders, George Stirrett was just one of many
connections based on a mutual interest in natural history.
Bill Emery returned to Toronto from his first visit to Pelee
with W.E. (June 1931) with thrilling stories he was eager to
share. He convinced James L. Baillie, curator of the Royal
Ontario Museum of Zoology (ROMZ), and Herb Southam,
an active naturalist from the Toronto area, to travel back
with him in early June 1932.[71] Years later, in a speech
addressed to the Toronto Ornithological Club, Baillie stated
that he had made sixty-one visits to Pelee over thirty-seven
years, most of these in the spring. Baillie maintained that it
was the best place in North America to watch spring migration and "as a place for occurrence of unexpected vagrants,
Point Pelee is unexcelled."[72] On April 15, 1938, sixteen-
year-old Harold Lancaster took his first trip to Point Pelee
with Earl Lemon. Lemon "called and asked if I would like
to go to Point Pelee where he arranged to meet members of
the London McIlwraith Club including Dr. W.E. Saunders.
Would I!?"[73] In 1955 William A. (Bill) Martin and a friend
attended a night course in ornithology at the University of
Toronto, taught by Baillie. He made it clear to the participants that if they visited Point Pelee National Park in May,
they would most likely get to see the birds he was describing. The following May, Martin set off to "see what the
place had to offer."[74]

James Baillie had another Great Lakes Ornithological

The original gateway to Point Pelee National Park, 1918.

Club connection in the person of Fleming. For several years, Fleming had been scouting for a suitable place to leave his extensive bird collection. In 1923, Lester Lynn Snyder, then a young gallery technician at the Royal Ontario Museum of Zoology, introduced himself to Fleming. In Snyder, Fleming found a kindred spirit. With the encouragement of Snyder, Fleming joined the Brodie Club, which was composed mainly of ROMZ staff, and eventually felt comfortable enough with the workings of the museum to leave his entire collection of books and bird skins there. James Baillie first became acquainted with Fleming through the Brodie Club and the Toronto Ornithological Club. In 1937, as cataloguer of birds at the ROMZ, Baillie was given the onerous task of cataloging and relabelling Fleming's collection and came to know him quite well.[75]

Fleming himself had a broad network of influence. He was well-travelled, attending such meetings as the International

Ornithological Congress in London, England, first in 1905 and later acting as official Canadian representative. He became a member of the American Ornithologists' Union and at a meeting in Quebec City, October 1933, was the first Canadian to be elected president. His term of office ended in 1935 at a meeting in Toronto, an appropriate city in which to finish as it allowed him to show his extensive bird collection to visiting members.[76] Fleming was a member of the Toronto Ornithological Club (inaugural meeting January 5, 1934) and the Brodie Club, where he presented forty-five papers.[77] He became a mentor for young naturalists such as Hoyes Lloyd, whom he helped place in charge of implementing the Migratory Birds Convention Act of 1917,[78] and it was mainly due to Fleming's lobbying efforts that Taverner was hired as ornithologist for the new Victoria Memorial Museum in Ottawa in March 1911.

As Taverner was not known in Ottawa, it was necessary to inform those responsible—Reginald Walter Brock, Director of the Geological Survey and Acting Deputy Minister of Mines, and John Macoun at the Geological Survey—that here was a young man capable of filling such an important role. Fleming, with the instincts of a natural lobbyist, made a visit to Ottawa where he became acquainted with Brock and discussed the possible appointment of Taverner, while W.E. wrote to John Macoun.[79] The outcome was a happy one for Taverner, who made his way to Ottawa in order to take up the position that he would hold for thirty-one years. In the meantime, he was aware of the fact that he owed his friends a great deal. Nor did he forget Point Pelee, the place where he had gained so much experience. In an article written for the *Ottawa Naturalist* in 1911, Taverner described the location of Point Pelee and then explained the use of the Point, along with the islands, as a natural migration passage across Lake Erie. He pointed out that birds normally known to travel as individuals, such as Sharp-shinned, Cooper's, Red-tailed, Red-shouldered and Rough-legged Hawks, and Northern Saw-whet Owls were seen to occur in "flocks" in the fall; that these gatherings are brought together by, and are the result of, "congestion of a wide migration front into the narrow bounds of the Point."[80] In 1915 Taverner presented a paper to the Conservation Commission's annual meeting in Ottawa requesting that Point Pelee be set aside as a national park; in 1918 this was done.

While introducing Point Pelee to Ottawa, Taverner was also busy writing a book called *The Birds of Eastern Canada* (published in 1919). That book had an impact on young birder Harrison F. Lewis, who went on to become the first Canadian to obtain a PhD in ornithology (from Cornell, 1929, under the supervision of Arthur A. Allen[81]). When the American Ornithologists' Union met at Detroit in 1931, Lewis was one of the AOU members to make the field trip to Point Pelee with W.E. Saunders.

The remaining Canadian member of the GLOC, Alfred Brooker Klugh, was more interested in the flora of Point Pelee, but he recognized the need for further study of the birds of the area. He was a very active member of the Wellington Field Naturalists Club of Guelph, serving as treasurer and then as editor of its journal, the *Ontario Natural Science Bulletin*. In 1906, he moved to Kingston, Ontario, where he received his MA in botany from Queen's University and went on to become a lecturer in their Department of Biology. He organized the Queen's University Naturalists' Club, contributed to the *Auk*, the

Canadian Field-Naturalist, and wrote a nature study column for the *Farmer's Advocate,* which was published in London, Ontario.[82] Although he died prematurely in an accident in 1932, his influence was already widespread through his club memberships, publications, and teaching.

The American contingent of the GLOC, Swales and Lynds Jones, brought information about Point Pelee south of the border through contacts in the many organizations to which they belonged, and through their writing about their experiences in nature study publications. Swales moved to Washington, DC, in 1918 where he was appointed honorary custodian of birds' eggs in the National Museum. In 1921, he was appointed honorary assistant curator of birds. Swales became an associate member of the AOU in 1902, and a full member in 1909. He was a member of the Cooper Ornithological Club in 1898, a member and later vice-president of the Wilson Ornithological Club in 1903. Swales was a member of the Delaware Valley Ornithological Club and a founder of the Baird Ornithological Club in 1922, as well as its president at the time of his death in 1928. By that time he had just over one hundred articles published, including "The Birds of Point Pelee," of which he was co-author.[83]

Jones taught a course in ornithology at Oberlin College, Ohio, and belonged to the Wilson Ornithological Club, where he served as editor of the *Wilson Bulletin,* and in the capacity of president from 1927-1929. As editor of the bulletin, Jones published the findings of Norman A. Wood after his collecting trip for the University of Michigan Museum to Point Pelee in 1909. In that article Wood wrote:

> As may be inferred from the literature, Point
> Pelee is a very interesting region to the student

of bird migration. Descriptions, however, while giving the facts, cannot do the subject justice and fortunate is the observer who has an opportunity of watching the migrating hordes of birds that assemble and cross Lake Erie at this place.[84]

Thus, through organizations, word of mouth and published articles, the star that was Point Pelee also began to rise on the American horizon.

For birders, to read about Point Pelee was to aspire to go there. One such young naturalist from Ingersoll, who finally made it to the Point September 4, 1949: "Reading everything I could about birds and nature and Federation of Ontario Naturalists Club meetings and going to field events, Point Pelee was often mentioned in such glowing terms I looked forward to the day when I could visit and bird this interesting area."[85]

This simple statement expresses the very essence of what the GLOC members tried so hard, and so successfully, to accomplish. They began with a desire to learn more about the Great Lakes Region. As it happened, they explored a special location, discovered new information concerning migration, did some much needed collecting, and compiled an annotated checklist of birds, all the while encouraging other serious naturalists to join them in the study of this fascinating place. Point Pelee owes much to the men in the photograph. They, in turn, owe much to Point Pelee.

CHAPTER 4
Exploitation

By the late 1800s North American governments were scrambling to get a better understanding of the natural resources within their jurisdiction, while museums and universities were clamouring for display and research specimens. In the mid-1800s American ornithologist Elliot Coues wrote a letter to Montague Chamberlain, an ornithologist from Saint John, New Brunswick, in which he says: "I ... trust you will not take it amiss if I call your attention to the great amount of work that needs to be done before your country can stand side by side with the United States in this branch of science."[86] This kind of condescension by American ornithologists spurred on the Canadians, such as Dr. William Brodie, who had an interest in the field. Brodie, having been appointed the first provincial biologist in the Ontario Provincial Museum in 1903, was aware that the United States had a better developed system of museums. A collector himself, he knew that Coues' criticism was justified, and he therefore encouraged Canadians such as Fleming to carry on with this important work. His own specimens would eventually become part of the Toronto Normal School Museum's collection. It was Brodie's understanding that collecting bird specimens was a necessary evil, and that once a complete set was obtained, the need would become nonexistent.

Brodie knew that the Geological Survey of Canada, founded in 1842, was the only federal institution involved in natural history research. It had been set up in order to find, name, and compile information on all Canadian natural resources. This was done mainly for the sake of exploitation by both government and private interests; the focus therefore was on minerals, trees, fish, and fur-bearing animals. The Geological Survey was headquartered in Montreal under the directorship of William Henry Logan, who established a museum of geological specimens. A new mandate moved the Survey to Ottawa in 1881 and included less utilitarian branches of natural history such as botany. John Macoun, a professor of botany and geology at Albert College in Belleville, Ontario, was appointed to the position of Dominion botanist with the Geological Survey. Macoun's responsibility was "identifying potential areas for agriculture expansion."[87]

Under that direction, on June 29 and 30, 1882, John Macoun, accompanied by his son James Macoun, Professor William Saunders (father of W.E.) of London, and Dr. Burgess, examined the botanical features of the western peninsula of Ontario, "from the head of Lake Erie to the Niagara River."[88] There is nothing in the official report regarding collections, but William Saunders wrote an article in the *Canadian Entomologist* in which he described some of their findings: "We saw more Dragon-flies and other Neuropterous insects than we had ever seen in our lives before."[89] Among those insects were an Olive Hairstreak and a Mexican Sulphur; two new butterfly records for Canada. Macoun returned to Point Pelee in 1884 in order to collect tree samples for a British exhibition,[90] and the annual report of the Geological Survey of Canada describes another trip to Point Pelee in May 1901. During that trip Macoun and his party also spent time on Pelee Island, and visited Amherstburg, Windsor, Sandwich, Wallaceburg and Sarnia. Macoun noted that specimens of Blue Ash (*Fraxinus quadrangulata*), and Honey Locust (*Gleditsia triacanthos*) were seen at Point Pelee, and Northern Hackberry (*Celtis occidentalis*) occupied "more than half the area on some parts of the point."[91] Little is mentioned in this particular report about other aspects of the natural history of the area, and the list of specimens only mentions plants.

The fact that the Geological Survey focused mainly on opportunities for wealth was not lost on Canadian naturalists. In a letter to the editor of the *Canadian Sportsman* and *Naturalist*, in 1883, Thomas McIlwraith, an ornithologist from Hamilton, Ontario, wrote:

> At the present time, when so much excitement prevails at home and abroad, regarding the prospect wealth of our country, and when so much capital and energy are being expended in developing its resources, it is pleasant to notice that those branches of its Natural History which are not directly associated with the acquisition of wealth, are not being forgotten, and that while hundreds are striving to gain possession of the most productive lands, the richest mineral deposits or the most valuable timber limits, a quieter class of workers are equally busily engaged collecting, and identifying such specimens of Natural History as come within the range of their observations through-

out the country; the results of their researches are being placed on record, and when the excitement attendant on the first settlement of the new country now being opened up, has subsided, it will be a pleasant pastime for the rising generation to read therein the names and habits of the beautiful birds and flowers which surround their homes.[92]

The "quieter class of workers" would include Fleming, W.E. Saunders, Taverner, Keays, and Wallace, working at Point Pelee because it readily provided them with unexpected species as well as large numbers of more common birds.

Ornithologists were well aware of the fact that rare sightings were not accepted without an accompanying specimen, forcing them into the role of collectors and making collecting an activity essential to becoming known as a serious scientist.

On September 15, 1905, at the Tip of Point Pelee, Taverner, Swales, and Klugh collected a bird unknown to any of them and brought it back to camp in order to compare it with Coues' *Key to North American Birds*—the best resource available to them at the time. Taverner and Swales believed the specimen to be a Red Knot but agreed that there was a need to check further by looking at skins and collections.[93] Identification difficulties of this sort made collections indispensable. Finding new birds such as the Red Knot also led Taverner to hold forth on the advantages of visiting Point Pelee, as he did after a trip September 1, 1906:

Pelee upheld its old reputation as a bird ground
and we met several new species, some new for
the Point others new to us and one new to
Canada. We never go to Point Pelee without
something interesting happening. We secured
a good line of skins and increased our collections with a lot of most desirable stuff—among
which is some duck skins that Gardiner shot on
the marsh and gave to us. ... Connecticuts were
very much in evidence. Of course they took
looking for but we could have gotten many
more than we did if we had had a mind to. We
brought seven home. ... The greatest take of
the trip however was a Blue-winged warbler—
making a first record for the Dominion.[94]

The new birds were important for these young ornithologists who were hoping to make their reputations and
eventually be accepted amongst the elite of the North
American birding world. To that end Taverner and Swales
worked diligently, while around them a storm was gathering.

The storm had its roots in the 1839 Upper Canada game
laws establishing a closed season on a number of game bird
species. Those laws were rewritten and extended to include
fur-bearing animals in 1856 and, by 1864, insectivorous and
other small birds regarded as beneficial to farmers' crops were
also protected through legislation. The British North America
Act placed natural resources under provincial jurisdiction, and
after hearing a report from the Royal Commission on Fish and
Game, Ontario strengthened its Game and Fish Acts and set
up a new Game and Fisheries Board. By 1892 there were 392
deputy game wardens in Ontario. At the annual meeting of the

North American Fish and Game Protective Association in 1902, Edwin Tinsley, Ontario's chief game warden, stated: "There is not one redeeming feature or valid excuse for otherwise intelligent people acting so foolishly as to shoot birds when full of eggs en route to the nesting grounds."[95] Tinsley did not see any justification for killing birds in the spring and was not adverse to making things uncomfortable for those who did it.

By 1906, in spite of the obvious need for collections in Canada, and in face of the accolades coming from the United States for the work now being done,[96] there was a backlash against gathering specimens. This was coming from citizens and humane societies who blamed hunters for the extinction of the Passenger Pigeon (at Point Pelee the last ones were reported in 1882, and in North America the last one died in captivity in the Cincinnati Zoological Garden on September 1, 1914) and saw collecting as cruel and unnecessary. In a letter to Fleming, March 22, 1907, Taverner describes his shock at being, for the first time in his life, approached by the local game warden concerning his collecting permit. Again that year, October 12, Taverner told Fleming that the game warden drove out to check their permits and warned them not to shoot at a mark, even on Sundays. Taverner thought that someone from Leamington complained: "They cannot understand any one preferring to shoot small birds instead of ducks. ... Am afraid that some of them will write to Tinsley and he may not issue me with a permit next year in consequence."[97] A suggestion came from W.E. Saunders that he obtain a Michigan permit first, thereby lending weight to his request for a local permit. Taverner followed this advice and received an Ontario permit without difficulty.

Brodie and Fleming, trying to explain the reasons for

Percy Taverner climbing the survey tower at the Tip of Point Pelee, 1909.

collecting, argued that in gaining a better understanding of birds through specimens, and using them to instruct young men and women, they were, in fact, saving other species from the same fate as the Passenger Pigeon. Yet, upon reading passages such as these in letters from Taverner to Fleming, one wonders at the legitimacy of that argument: "The Rough-wings we got were young birds. Did not really take fullest advantage of our opportunities as I got but two or three specimens. Could have got dozens as well as not." Another letter stated, "You missed a great sight at the Point. A flight of Saw-whet Owls. At least in consideration of the rarity of the species I think it could be called a flight. We shot nine of them in less than two hours and only quit looking for them because we had enough."[98] But in spite of the impression left by these statements made by Taverner, he did not agree with wanton destruction and his enjoyment of nature would prevent him, with a few exceptions, from harvesting unnecessarily: "a single specimen that I saw having one single ruby feather in the middle of the throat. I should have collected the latter but it sat on a branch not five feet from me preening its feathers and acting so unconcerned that I had not the heart to do so."[99] While watching a flight of Purple Martins, August 27, 1907, Taverner again shows this sensitivity. At that time, there was a fifteen-metre observation tower with platform near the end of the Point, built by engineers involved in the study of the Lake Erie shoreline. This platform allowed the ornithologists to watch bird movement from a much higher vantage point, as is described by Taverner in the following paragraph:

> The sky was leaden in colour. Through the mist came the Martins. We were elevated to their plane of flight and were alone with them. On they came, bird after bird, on their strong bowed wings, out of the nebulous north, cutting strong and black against the neutral background. Without hurry or haste, calm, dignified and determined, they held a true course and swerved neither to one side or the other.[100]

Taverner's own awe at the sight was not shared by the local inhabitant who boasted of having killed seventeen in one shot. It is not surprising then, that for some citizens, "collecting" and "destroying" were one and the same, and they'd had enough.

The willingness of some Point Pelee residents to collect for outsiders highlights a continuous—even encouraged—process of exploitation of both local resources and inhabitants. W.E., obviously understanding the problem, used his considerable tact in an effort to teach the locals: "Two specimens were shot there by the kindhearted residents who knew my desire for rare specimens, but the little lecture that went with each note of thanks checked further killing and Mockingbirds are now greeted in other ways than by the shotgun."[101] W.E. recognized the need to remind them that more is not necessarily better, while at the same time appreciating rare specimens such as a White-winged Crossbill in a "box of birds from friends on the Point." The naturalists did not like needless destruction, but in the case where a number of a flock of Evening Grosbeak were killed by boys, their biggest concern was that they "were unable to get sight of any specimens." [102]

By 1911, the Geological Survey's Victoria Memorial Museum had just been completed in Ottawa and R.W. Brock, director of the Survey at the time, planned to make it a national museum that would reflect Canada as those south of the border did the United States: "The Department shall maintain a Museum of Geology and Natural History for the purpose of affording a complete and exact knowledge of the geology, mineralogy and mining resources of Canada ... collect, classify and arrange for exhibition in the Victoria Memorial Museum such specimens as are necessary to afford a complete and exact knowledge of the geology, mineralogy, paleontology, ethnology and fauna and flora of Canada."[103] Taverner, who had been appointed that same year as ornithologist at the Victoria Memorial Museum, set out for Ottawa where he would try to carry out the work mandated by Brock.

A couple of years later, May 15, 1913, he was back at Point Pelee, this time leading a collecting expedition from the Victoria Memorial Museum. The museum party, composed of Entomologist and Assistant to the Curator Charles H. Young, Chief Taxidermist Clyde L. Patch, and Taverner, remained on the Point for two and a half months.

For Taverner, "the most salient features ... worthy of record:"[104] A Northern Mockingbird pair nesting near a farmhouse was the only pair known in Canada. Three pairs of Lark Sparrow were also nesting close to the camp with at least one brood of fledglings sighted. Taverner considered that the breeding populations of Chipping Sparrow, Eastern Wood-Pewee, and Baltimore and Orchard Orioles were large. Northern Cardinals were in good numbers but the Carolina Wren went unheard throughout their stay. Taverner was amazed by the numbers of Lincoln Sparrows seen in only two days, and believed that they would have found more given more time to study them. Philadelphia and Warbling Vireo were common. On May 19, a male Prothonotary Warbler was collected—only the third positive record for Canada backed up by a specimen. Two Least Bittern were seen and collected. An Orange-crowned Warbler was taken. Several pairs of Sedge Wren were located but no nests found. Returning fall migrants seen passing through were Least Sandpiper, Semipalmated Plover, Yellowlegs, and Whimbrel. Fleming, Wallace, and W.E. Saunders joined Taverner and his workers at Point Pelee, during which time W.E. managed to secure a Hooded Warbler, the first one caught by him. He also collected a White-eyed Vireo, Lark Sparrow, and a male Golden-winged Warbler.[105] Since this trip was undertaken in order to collect material for large landscape displays in the museum, Taverner included a number of interesting butterflies and moths such as Olive Hairstreak, Zebra Swallowtail, Orange Sulphur, American Snout-Butterfly, and Common Buckeye. In a report of the trip, he notes the fact that Pawpaw, the larval food plant for Zebra Swallowtail, is nonexistent on the Point and wonders about the relative abundance of this species:

> One of the most interesting occurrences,
> however, in this line was the comparative
> abundance of Papilio ajax [Zebra Swallowtail].
> ... The commonly given food plant for this
> showy butterfly is the Pawpaw. This, however,
> does not occur on the Point and the nearest
> clump of it is more than six miles [10 kilome-
> tres] away across a wide marsh, yet we saw the
> species nearly every day and often from two to
> six. They flew swiftly and were difficult to
> capture. Those we managed to take were in
> almost unworn condition and the majority of
> those seen were perfect even to the ends of
> their long tails. It hardly seems possible that all
> of these should be wanderers from the little
> clump of Pawpaw in the main land and proba-
> bly the species has another food plant on the
> Point.[106]

This was the only collecting trip made to Point Pelee by
the Victoria Memorial Museum; subsequent trips were
made by the Royal Ontario Museum of Zoology, which had
been established in 1912. Both the Victoria Memorial
Museum and the Royal Ontario Museum of Zoology
carried out their own trips in order to acquire specimens for
their particular needs. By the 1930s, with the museums
doing this work, private collectors like Fleming, who had
amassed enough specimens to use for systematic study, were
no longer necessary and gradually quit collecting. Most of
them donated their collections to one museum or the other.

Meanwhile, the world of bird observation was changing. By 1922 the majority of birdwatchers were using field glasses rather than guns.[107] Birdwatching had come a long way from Elliot Coues' view in 1874 that the "double barreled shot gun is your main reliance ... and ... evidence of your industry and ability."[108] Now birdwatchers were becoming satisfied with possessing the bird in the sense of knowing its nature, behaviour, and habitat. Of the ornithologists visiting Point Pelee, Fleming, writing to Taverner, September 26, 1907, was the first to mention a desire to turn his attention toward watching and recording using only glasses and a notebook.

More recently, birds killed for scientific purposes were sent directly to a nearby museum, but private collectors had the option of donating their specimens wherever they wished. A naturalist would need to apply for a special permit to collect in a national park; however, it is still possible to acquire one for specific study. Examples of continued collecting at Point Pelee are a Mountain Bluebird and a Bell's Vireo. The Mountain Bluebird was one of two females reported by Wilf Botham on December 4, 1965, and collected December 6 by William Wyett, Point Pelee National Park naturalist. Thus, positive identification through collection confirmed the occurrence of Mountain Bluebird in Ontario; the specimen is number 97,005 in the ROM.[109] The Bell's Vireo was collected June 23, 1970, again by William Wyett, and became specimen number 57,428 in the Canadian Museum of Nature (formerly the Victoria Memorial Museum).[110] The collection of these specimens was deemed acceptable because of their educational value. As early as 1958, the ongoing controversy over the collection of specimens forced curator Lester L. Snyder to defend and explain the position of the Royal Ontario Museum:

> Over the last ten years the museum has collected exactly 13 specimens which would classify as regional rarities, waifs and possible pioneers. One proves the first and only occurrence of a species for the whole of Canada. Two represent European species having no breeding outposts in the New World and the chances of these individuals reaching home would seem slight. Five were hybrids, the living existence of which could have meant nothing to the parent species. Two proved that previous field identification of them by local observers was incorrect. The other three were important for various reasons including sole age and plumage representation for the province.[111]

At Point Pelee, where rare birds turn up with some regularity and growing numbers of birders were interested in seeing them, the consensus was against collecting. Birders did not appreciate travelling down to Point Pelee to see a reported rarity just to find out that the object of their visit had been shot. Today, although some formal collecting still takes place, birds that end up in museums as specimens from Point Pelee are birds that are found dead but in good condition, such as those that fly into a window, get hit by a car, or expire due to severe weather conditions.

CHAPTER 5

Bird Banding

Amber eyes glowed, unblinking, stubbornly hiding secrets and demanding freedom. For an instant Sarah stared back, her skin prickling with apprehension; then, rubbing the sleep from her eyes, she sighed in relief. A Northern Saw-whet Owl was being held by her father, whose large hands further dwarfed the tiny brown bird. Soft white feathering above a curved beak spread upwards into the facial discs around those eyes, catching the pale light of the banding cabin and reflecting it back in a vague v-shaped shimmer. The white breast was streaked with soft rust that disappeared into the darker brown of side and wings. Dennis F. Rupert popped the little bird into a canister in order to weigh it, and wrote a number in the blue three-ringed binder. Sliding it back out into his hand, he spread one wing, showing Sarah white-tipped feathers on brown background. Next, the tail of the Saw-whet Owl was measured and a tiny metal band was clamped around its lower leg to complete the process. Sarah watched her father's deft movements in fascination. The little owl would soon be free to continue his interrupted journey. As her father headed back out into that cold October night in 1973, Sarah shivered and pulled the coarse blanket up to her chin. Settling back on the old camp cot, she slowly relaxed and dreamed of a time when she would be old enough to work by his side.

Sarah Rupert, who went on to become a senior park interpreter at Point Pelee National Park, was not the first person to dream of bird banding here. In a letter to Fleming, October 12, 1907, Percy Taverner allowed himself to do some wishful thinking of his own: "With a very little continuous work Point Pelee could be made as classical a ground as Heligoland." Heligoland is a German island in the North Sea where a successful banding station had been in operation since 1891. Here studies were already being done on migration using a trap developed by the islanders to catch thrushes.112 Taverner felt that had he been a good speaker he could have raised the funds needed to establish a station on Point Pelee, but he was burdened with a stutter. Instead, in an attempt to get the ball rolling, he wrote articles discussing the advantages of tagging birds in order to gain information about their movements. Also, between 1905 and 1908, he fashioned about four hundred bird bands, which he gave to several of his ornithologist friends. One of these would ring the leg of an American Robin, the first bird to be banded in Canada. Fleming would be the bander and the location would be his back yard at 267 Rusholme Road, Toronto, September 24, 1905.

Although Taverner was banding land birds and Jack Miner was banding waterfowl, these activities were small scale, and not connected to any other banding that might have been going on at the time. This was remedied in 1909 with the organization of the American Bird Banding Association and the election of Leon J. Cole as its first president. The Bird Banding Association organized the banders, provided the bands, and dealt with the resultant paper work until 1911, when the Linnean Society of New York took on the financial obligations of bird banding. In 1920, the work had outgrown the American Bird Banding Association and all the responsibilities associated with banding went to the Bureau of Biological Survey of the US Department of Agriculture in Washington, DC, and all records for the continent were to be kept in Washington.

The Canadian bird-banding program officially started in 1923 when Canada agreed to work co-operatively with the United States. It fell within the purview of the Dominion Parks Branch under Supervisor of Wildlife Protection Hoyes Lloyd, whose department recorded data and issued standardized bands. Lloyd wrote an article which appeared in the *Canadian Field-Naturalist*, recommending Point Pelee as a location to set up a banding station. He cited the fact that it was a migration highway so, with a concerted effort, would surely turn up a great deal of information. He made it quite plain to all interested naturalists that they could expect the "co-operation of the Canadian National Parks service ... because it is in this branch of the Interior Department that all Canadian banding records are kept."[113] This offer of support was in itself a message of encouragement to those who might be interested. Unfortunately, in 1927, when the article appeared, there was no organization with enough members, time, or money to take on the task.

When conditions finally coalesced to allow bird banding to begin at Point Pelee, the "organization" would be a loosely knit group of birders, mostly from the Toronto area. The organizer was William W. H. Gunn. The catalyst was reverse migration—birds flying south in the spring when they should be flying north, and flying north in the fall when they should be flying south. This unusual activity can easily be seen at the Tip of Point Pelee and is a phenomenon that leaves watchers in awe.

It is May 9, 2002. As on any May morning, hundreds of birders crowd the Tip of Point Pelee. Suddenly, scopes are forgotten where they stand. Binoculars are held up to the eyes with freezing fingers. No one moves. Dark, writhing, twisting, ever-moving flocks of birds travel south over the last trees, over the sandspit reaching far into the lake, and away to the south and southwest. They consist of warblers, woodpeckers, blackbirds, orioles, grosbeaks, and more.

The birds come in waves as large as hundreds or groups as small as five or six, but they come, as inexorable and unstoppable as a tornado. Some land in trees to the north of the Tip and flit from branch to branch, tree to tree, finally, with a burst of energy, pushing off over Lake Erie to disappear into a horizon of blue sky and lake. Others wing their course far overhead, neither hesitating nor dropping down, oblivious of the watchers who are in awe below. Against all reason, for upwards to three hours that parade of size, shape, and colour continues.

Reverse migration in all its mystery is an unforgettable sight; no one who experiences it is left untouched

Dr. Harrison F. Lewis, federal migratory bird officer for Ontario and Quebec, first observed reverse migration in the early morning of May 12, 1937. He was on Pelee Island when he noticed that some birds at Fish Point were actually flying south when they should have been flying north. Lewis began researching reverse migration, reading as much as he could and trying to piece together the reasons for this unusual behaviour. He soon found out that spring reverse migration at Point Pelee was first recorded by W.E. Saunders, March 13, 1909, when he became aware of House

Sparrows flying south.[114] B.H. Swales describes reverse migration of Ruby-throated Hummingbirds May 7 of that same year. On April 10, 1915, W.E. again noted a "strong tendency for southern migration, all blackbirds, house sparrows, flickers, bluebirds and robins disappear to the south. Some of the Blackbird flocks are as large as 200 birds."[115] Curious and determined to find out more, Dr. Lewis visited Point Pelee for four days in April 1938. There he saw reverse migration at the Tip with Barn Swallows, European Starlings, House Sparrows, and blackbirds flying south. In a letter to Lester L. Snyder, Dr. Lewis attempted to interest the Toronto ornithologists in a co-operative study of the area. He suggested setting up research stations on Point Pelee, Pelee Island, and in Ohio, "On account of the discontinuous character of the land to be traversed it offers a number of concentration points a few miles apart. ... The route provides seven first-class observation points, four in Ontario and three in Ohio." The plan was a good one but the timing was bad. There was no money available for a study, so observers would be unpaid as well as responsible for their own travel and living expenses. Added to that, while Point Pelee was a fairly accessible location, some of the others were not. Pelee Island had only intermittent and expensive ferry service, while Middle Island was privately owned and one needed to get permission in writing before working there. Also since unpaid volunteers could only make themselves available on weekends and holidays, it was difficult to have enough people at their stations simultaneously. And war took its toll on the project as well. Ornithologists were joining the armed forces and gasoline was rationed.

Nevertheless, Lewis' enthusiasm generated enough interest to encourage William W. H. Gunn, then at the University of Toronto, to make reverse migration the subject of his doctoral thesis. Work began, albeit on a much reduced scale, in May 1939. As Hoyes Lloyd had indicated they would be several years earlier, park personnel were co-operative, allowing Gunn's "team" to use the Life-saving Station as headquarters for the week of May 7. (The Life-saving Station was an empty three-story building originally belonging to the Department of Marine and Fisheries, located near the Tip and used at one time by members of the life-saving crew who were hired to watch for shipping accidents and rescue survivors.) There, in the bottom level boat house, Bill Emery and James Baillie, along with their wives, set up cots. Dr. Lewis spent some time with the group at Point Pelee, then went on to Middle Island and Fish Point, Pelee Island, to watch there, while Dr. W.E. Saunders joined the team at Point Pelee May 10. Lighthouse Point, South Bass Island, Long Point, and Kelleys Island were studied during that same week by K. H. Doan and Dr. C. F. Walker of Put-in-Bay, Ohio. Coverage continued to be fairly good for May of 1940 with Dr. Harrison F. Lewis and William W. H. Gunn leading a team which consisted of fellow naturalists Ron Bremner, John MacArthur, Doug Miller, Dr. Robert Ritchie, John A. Livingston, David N. Scott, Don MacDonald, and Richard D. Ussher from Toronto, and William G. Girling from London, all involved in watching at Point Pelee.

A fourteen-day migration watch and banding trip took place May 1941, with William Gunn, Bill Emery, Terry Shortt, George W. North, and James Baillie its participants. Post House, situated within easy walking distance of the Tip and on the northwest corner of a large open area, now known as the Sparrow Field, became their headquarters for that trip. This huge, vacant, concrete-block building had been bought by the Park a couple of years before and renovated as tourist accommodations in 1939. It proved to be an excellent place to stay, with hardwood flooring and a screened-in porch. Park picnic tables and benches were used for furniture and the superintendent kindly lent them a stove. All their gear had been sent on ahead of them to Wallace Tilden, a Point Pelee native and farmer. Gunn and his colleagues arrived at Point Pelee at 2:00 a.m., waking the superintendent to acquire a key to the house and causing a stir in the Tilden household in order to obtain their equipment. On that trip banding small birds was one method of study used by Gunn. He had fashioned a trap out of a green wire cage, 90 centimetres long, 60 centimetres wide and 90 centimetres deep. A kettle hanging from a branch above dripped water into a pan inside the cage, attracting the attention of small birds. A door at the top and another at one end were attached to string and manipulated by the bander from his hideout.[116] Don MacDonald, who had been involved with Gunn's research the previous year, was birding at Point Pelee with some friends during this time. He records having seen a banded White-crowned Sparrow near some lilac bushes by Post House, and spending time at the trap where he "watched Bill Gunn banding a male Wilson's Warbler."[117] This was his first experience with banding, and a sure indication that Gunn's trap was working.

Unfortunately, the next five years reflected the fact that the world was at war. No studies were done in 1942, although Gunn, accompanied by his wife, conducted subsequent spring watches. It was 1947 before Bill Emery again helped him, with George North, Bruce Falls, W. Giles, and

William W. H. Gunn releasing a White-crowned Sparrow after banding it at Point Pelee, May 1941.

Robert Ritchie as observers in May 1948. Only Bruce Falls, K. Mayall, and Gunn worked in 1949 with a much larger contingent—James Baillie, along with A. Glendenning, Keith Reynolds (London), and Mrs. Sisman and Mrs. Williams (Aurora)—helping to cover days in both April and May in 1950, the last year of Gunn's research.

For the record, Dr. Gunn's findings about reverse migration are as follows:

1) Strongest reverse migration was seen from the Tip of Point Pelee and Fish Point, Pelee Island.

2) It occurred at a rate of more than 180 birds per hour on thirty-one per cent of the May watches and twelve per cent of April watches.

3) It was most evident between one and four hours after sunrise.

4) Seventy-one species, largely passerines, were involved.

5) A strong correlation existed between the intensity of southward flight and the condition of the weather. Southward flight is heavy when the region is overlain by the west side of a high pressure area or the warm sector of a low pressure area: conversely, it is light when the region is overlain by the east side of a high or the western or northern portions of a low. Heavier flights thus usually occur with rising temperatures, falling pressure, and winds more or less adverse.

6) Complex impulses are involved which were identified as: reaction to climatic ecological conditions found upon arrival in the region; post-migration wandering; avoidance of existing or approaching inclement weather; and a tendency to fly against the wind.

The concentration of numbers and flight direction toward the south are thought to be strongly accentuated by the topographical influence of the funnel-like, southward-directed points of land at Point Pelee and Fishing Point, Pelee Island.[118]

With reverse migration studies complete, Ontario ornithologists were ready to put their energy into a new project. And the Federation of Ontario Naturalists was ready to support them. As early as 1935, George North had been in Essex County, at the request of the Federation of Ontario Naturalists, to report on the numbers of hawks passing through various points of the peninsula. This organization was quite open to the suggestion of a bird-banding station, and Point Pelee, with its great concentration of migrant birds in both spring and fall, was the obvious location. In 1953, a formal request to establish a bird-banding station at Point Pelee was presented to the Federation of Ontario Naturalists by five members of the Toronto Intermediate Naturalists, a club that met at the ROM in the 1940s and early 1950s, and was mentored by Jim Baillie, Don Burton, Hugh Curr, George Francis, Michael Porter and Jim Woodford. Their proposal was on the Board of Director's agenda for March 6, 1954. It is no surprise that Dr. William Gunn, who was also a member of the FON, was an advocate for the proposal, stating that migration of songbirds and other small land birds was an area in need of further study and that such a station at Point Pelee would likely be the "first of its type in North America."[119]

Money seemed to be a major factor in the decision-making process, but since $500.00 of the estimated $750.00 that was needed would come from the Point Pelee National Park Advisory Committee, the proposal was approved. Permission was granted by both the National Parks Branch and the Canadian Wildlife Service. February of 1955 saw Mike Porter (who had experience with Heligoland traps in England), George Francis, and Jim Woodford staking out the outline for the Heligoland trap near the last vegetation on the Point. The Heligoland trap consisted of a large, 12 metre long, tapered wire netting enclosure with an entrance that was 11 metres wide and 6 metres high. The closed end was a metre wide and two metres high, with a sharp curve to one side. Here, a ramp leading up to a collecting box encourages birds to enter the upper section of the two-tiered structure. Once they have done so, a sloping glass plate appears to them as a means of escape. In truth, it induces them to enter the lower level where a door in the side of the collecting box is used for their removal.

Dr. Gunn, who had been hired by the FON to get the banding project off the ground, and his cadre of volunteers had the trap built and ready to operate by May 9.

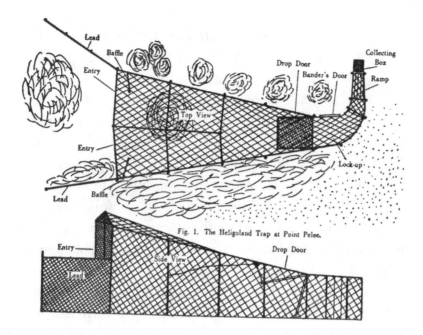

Fig. 1. The Heligoland Trap at Point Pelee.

The Heligoland trap at Point Pelee, 1954.

Unfortunately, because Francis, Woodford, and Porter were unable to be there, the trap ended up being built near the traffic circle instead of where they had planned. This turned out to be a rather poor location. Inclement weather also slowed down the work, with the result that only 205 birds of 38 species had been banded by May 29. The trap was then dismantled and stored at Point Pelee National Park for future use.

Banding was a new endeavour for all the volunteers, so it was very much trial and error that first year. Banders themselves became more efficient, beginning with an average banding rate of twenty to twenty-five per cent of all birds entering the trap and finishing the season with a seventy-five to eighty per cent success rate. During the course of the first season changes were made to the Heligoland trap in order to make it more effective. Experience from that first season gave banders many ideas for improvements. Suggestions made included further modifications for the Heligoland trap, that auxiliary trapping methods such as mist nets be used, that qualified volunteers be used, and that trapping start earlier in the season. It was also suggested that more data be collected: that trapped birds be weighed and measured and that records of temperatures and rainfall be kept. Many of these recommendations were followed, and banders also began recording the age and sex of each subject in an attempt to discover if juveniles, males, and females migrated on different schedules. A common station band was issued and used. While this last change did not sit well with some banders who were using their own bands, it became standard practice. Recalling these early days, Jim Woodford speaks of Pelee as a "pioneer station that really got co-operative banding going in Canada."[120]

Japanese mist nets were added to the banding equipment being used at Pelee in 1955. Unlike the trap, which was stationary, these nets could be moved from one location to another depending on the wind and weather conditions. They could also be shifted quickly to take advantage of temporary local movements of birds. They proved to be a success, with over 250 Black-capped Chickadees alone captured by them in a single day. With improved weather conditions and use of mist nets, totals rose to eight hundred birds banded and several recaptured from 1954.

In those early years, as it is today, the dedication of volunteer banders was essential to the success of the station: the wake-up call came at 4:00 a.m. and breakfast was a hurried affair sipped from the lip of a chipped and stained coffee cup. Real food would have to wait. Out-of-doors before dawn, bird banders scurried to prepare for the morning, oblivious to the beauty of ropes of spider webs carrying mist from tree to tree. Cold droplets on forearm or neck send a chilly message that this is still only May. At the Heligoland trap, a young man walks through the gloom of early morning, around the fenced-in enclosure, scanning for small animals, holes, or damage done by deer. He vividly recalls a time when a skunk was busy digging for grubs one morning, but today all is clear. He finally reaches the closed end where he replaces the glass plate that had been removed by a bander at the end of the previous day in order to allow birds to pass through while the trap was not being monitored. Now the trap is ready for the reverse migrants moving south along the Point. His helper will arrive from Leamington momentarily. For now, the bander can relax.

Meanwhile, slightly north and east of him, a man and his wife work side by side to set the mist nets into position. They have decided that all nets should be on the east side of the Point where Lake Erie lies calm and glassy. Just inside the woods, several lanes have been chopped out of the underbrush and grape tangles. Here the nine-metre long, two-metre high, silk mist nets with their three-and-three-quarter-centimetre stretched mesh, will do best, catching up small warblers and the like. The stronger, nylon six-and-a-quarter-centimetre stretched mesh nets are still in the banding cabin. Today banders will concentrate on small land birds. The bottom half of the three-metre, steel electrical conduit poles are pounded into the soft Pelee sand; the upper half, with the net attached, is placed on top and joined by a standard connector. Finally, the four shelf-string loops are slipped over the pole with the top string looped tight enough to prevent slipping. All

is ready as a glorious sun rises over Lake Erie. No one
watches sunrise here, however. Eyes riveted, hands ready,
the mist nets hold all their attention. Bird movement
begins, tension mounts.

Several of these avid banders went on to form the
Ontario Bird Banding Association (OBBA) during the
winter of 1955-56. The first executive consisted of Herb
Southam (president), Frank Lovesy (vice-president), Bill
Wasserfall (secretary-treasurer) and Jim Woodford, who
was appointed editor of a proposed newsletter. Their focus
was primarily improving coverage at the Point and developing a proposal for fall banding.

A description of banding at Point Pelee in May 1956,
written by Woodford in *Ontario Bird Banders' Association
Banding Newsletter*, gives some notion of the experiences
possible as well as the learning processes taking place during
the course of this fascinating, if unpredictable activity:

> The night of 12 May produced some unusual
> occurrences. Shortly after a severe squall, a
> tapping was heard on the door of the banders'
> cottage, and when the door was opened a
> White-crowned Sparrow flew in to be greeted
> by several astonished banders. After being
> caught and banded he spent the night on the
> verandah, and flew away in the morning none
> the worse for the unexpected hospitality. Plans
> had been made to try night banding, and it was
> discovered that the storm had forced down
> considerable numbers of Brown Thrashers,
> Catbirds and Empidonax Flycatchers which
> were perching in the larger trees ... the most

unusual being a Yellow Rail discovered perching in a small cedar 6 feet [two metres] from the ground. Jacklighting proved effective because of the darkness of the night. On later attempts it was found that on moonlight nights the birds would take off in moth-like flight when caught in the rays of the light.[121]

That spring the results were a record 2,837 birds representing 102 species banded in May at Point Pelee over twenty-eight days. Among those birds were a Least Flycatcher and a Barn Swallow that were caught again on Pelee Island in the mist nets Frank Lovesy and Jim Woodford were working. Of 1,400 birds banded on Pelee Island that May 1956, these two gave the first positive proof of reverse migration. At Point Pelee, autumn banding statistics for that year were 691 birds of 66 species in nineteen days.

It was May of that particularly successful year that Bill Martin made his first trip to Point Pelee to birdwatch. He came upon bander Wishart Campbell busily disengaging small birds from a mist net, banding them and letting them go. Campbell had his mist net set up at Marshview Picnic Area and he had just caught a Northern Cardinal, Lincoln's Sparrow, and a female Golden-winged Warbler. As Martin watched, the cardinal and warbler were released and the sparrow kept for further assessment by Dr. Gunn, who was at the Tip manning the Heligoland trap that was "catching birds as they moved south in their 'reverse' flow."[122] The experience must have left quite an impression on Martin, who continued to come to Pelee to bird and also went on to become treasurer of the OBBA, designing both their logo and that of the Long Point Bird Observatory in 1967.

Banders headed for Point Pelee in April 1957 in order to make more changes to the Heligoland trap. This party of volunteers included members from Toronto, Detroit, London, and St. Thomas. A prior meeting between Mr. McCarron, the park superintendent, and members of the OBBA had established that the steel framework of the Heligoland trap needed to be replaced. It was agreed that poles and timber would be supplied from salvaged wood in the park, while the wire and netting needed would be paid for by an FON grant. The group worked diligently getting the trap ready, but poor weather conditions meant that banding did not start immediately. That had to wait until the return trip, which began May 1 and lasted until May 26, bringing in 1,821 birds of 93 species. Banding also took place on twenty-one days spread throughout July, August, September, and October. This activity brought in 1,055 individuals of 88 species. Of all birds caught in the spring, swallows formed the majority; conversely, Swainson's Thrush and Sharp-shinned Hawk constituted the highest per cent in the fall. After four years 7,417 birds of 137 species had been banded and now the Federation of Ontario Naturalists and the OBBA began to compile and review the data. More banders were needed and the future of banding in Point Pelee looked bright.

Robert R. Taylor, who was by that time working with the banders at Point Pelee, recalled the players and the game:

> In my early teens I developed an interest in
> bird-banding through Frank Smith who was a
> naturalist, bird-carver, and bander. My pals
> Ted Warren and Jerry Anderson often went

Robert R. Taylor, bird bander, photographer, writer, and natural-ist from Manitoba makes the trip to Point Pelee every May.

with me and Frank and another bander, Gordon Lambert, to band Saw-whet Owls and Screech Owls.

My interest in banding also led me to a friendship with Dr. William Gunn who was operating a banding station at the Tip of Point Pelee. I was drawn to the Heligoland Trap, and soon I found myself going to Pelee as often as possible to help with the banding.

Dr. Gunn ... was always willing to share his knowledge with those who had a genuine interest. One of my memories of him was when we were observing migrant birds passing in front of the full moon as we peered through his telescope at the tip. I learned to tell a sparrow from a thrush through that scope, but Bill

Gunn's skills went far beyond that.

The banding era had many memorable experiences. We had banding stations at the tip, way up the east beach road by the marsh, up at the north west beach, near the Aviation Inn (where the Visitor Centre parking lot is located) and at the sparrow field where the old Point Pelee Lodge was located. We rented cabins and cottages at various locations throughout the park.

One rainy evening, about 1957, Doug Dow and I went out to jacklight birds at the tip. It was cold and we were getting coated in ice as the rain began to freeze. In the beam of our spotlight we found several shorebirds that were suffering the consequences of the weather, so we captured them and took them back to our cabin by the Point Pelee Lodge to warm them up and to keep them overnight. The nasty weather continued throughout the night and in the morning we were shocked by the sight of dozens of birds shivering and even dying as they lay sprawled out on the ground. Hurriedly we gathered up as many as we could and tried to save them by taking them into the warmth of our small cabin. I don't know how many birds were in the cabin but there were a lot. The species ranged from a tiny Ruby-throated Hummingbird to a considerably larger Double-crested Cormorant. There were a couple of Black-bellied Plovers, some Sanderlings and other shorebirds, a few tanagers, sparrows, warblers, vireos, and more. By the end of the day the weather had improved considerably and most of the rescued birds had recovered to the point where they could be released with some assurance of their survival. We didn't band any of them, we just wanted them to be free as quickly as possible so that they could look for some food. Many birds perished in that storm, but on warm days that followed there were lots of birds around Pelee and lots of song in the air.

Our banding excursions provided many interesting observations and experiences. One cold, rainy night Bill Wasserfall and I watched a "pinwheel" of Sanderlings on the beach at the tip as they shuffled around in a tight circle, pushing to get towards the centre of the circle for protection against the weather and forcing other birds to the outside. We could hardly believe what we were seeing. There must have been over a hundred birds in a space less than three feet in diameter. We took great care not to disturb them.

On another occasion I was walking back from the tip with a weak and bedraggled Cormorant in a packsack so that I could take it back to the cabin and try to improve its condition. Seeing a group of birders ahead I acted nonchalant as I passed by only to hear them all giggling behind my back. The Cormorant had stuck its head out of the packsack and was curi-

ously watching the birders. Of course, I had to
turn around and show them the bird and
explain what I was doing with it.[123]

Bird banding was a rewarding experience for those
involved, and at Point Pelee the activity had been ongoing
long enough to begin showing some interesting results.
However, for reasons unknown to the banders, in 1958,
Point Pelee National Park restricted banding to two areas,
one where the Heligoland trap was located at the Tip, and
the other along East Beach, north of the crossroad. Permits
were only issued to five banders who were permitted to
bring in other banders as "associates" to assist them. The
spring of that year was disappointing in terms of birds
banded as well. The number of individuals was only 1,246 of
86 species. The fall banding results were better, but the
Heligoland trap was vandalized that summer and was not
available for fall use. Most of the banding was done on East
Beach Road, which was proving to be an excellent site for
mist nets. Also for the first time at Point Pelee, an attempt
was made to band Northern Saw-whet Owls on the evening
of October 18, 1958. Just before dark, Bill Wasserfall, Doug
Dow, and Bob Taylor set up eight mist nets between the
road and West Beach, west of Aviation Inn. When the nets,
which were being inspected every half hour, were checked at
10:15 p.m. by Dow and Taylor, two Saw-whets were found.
At 3:45 a.m., one Saw-whet owl was caught in a pocket. The
rest of the night was unproductive, but the overall results
led the OBBA to plan Saw-whet banding on a larger scale in
the future. However, it was time to find a more suitable
place for OBBA operations and Long Point was chosen.
George Stirrett "recommended the bird banding project to

the Long Point Company, who controlled a large area of Long Point and he put W. J. R. [Bill] Wasserfall in touch with Company officials so that the final arrangements for the banding project could be made."[124]

Meanwhile, banding continued at Point Pelee but statistics for spring 1959 were down, possibly due to a shortage of volunteers. An article in the OBBA newsletter sent a reminder to banders that continuous coverage in May and September was important. But not everyone agreed with banding birds, so by 1960 the Tip was no longer a good place to work. Dissenters caused disruptions by standing in front of the mist nets in order to prevent birds from entering. Organizations such as the Detroit Audubon Society were split with both protesters and banders among their members. To add another dimension to these problems, visitation to the Park soared (703,282 per year by 1965[125]). Some of these people objected to bird banding on principle, and others, not understanding the work, just felt sorry for the bird caught in the net. The OBBA was told that it could no longer band at the Tip in April, May, September, and October, the months during which migration takes place and bird banding is normally done. This meant that the Heligoland trap had to be moved to another location within Point Pelee, where the banders could continue to work. Also, Aviation Inn had been purchased by the Park and all the OBBA's equipment stored there had to be removed. This work was accomplished that fall by volunteers such as Bill Martin, who helped move the "trailer and heavy, Dexion-framed Heligoland trap to a spot way up the east beach almost to the cut at Cranberry Pond. The stable flies made the trip a misery."[126]

That year the OBBA meeting was held in September at the

banders' cottage on Don Tilden's farm at Point Pelee. Two decisions made during that weekend concerned the Point Pelee station. The first put John Roberts of Sarnia in charge of banding with help from Neil and Alice Kelley, the second was that all banding would have to be done by people from southwestern Ontario and adjacent Michigan. As luck would have it, there was an unusually large migration of Sharp-shinned Hawks taking place that Saturday and, working with only two nets, 170 hawks were banded by 11:00 a.m. and another 22 by evening. The following day, five nets were set up, resulting in 56 Sharp-shinned Hawks—some returnees from the day before—and 50 small birds being banded before 10:00 a.m., at which time members had to head for home. Of note was the fact that of 246 hawks banded, only two were in adult plumage and both were female.[127]

Banders must have been at a premium, as banding at Point Pelee was confined to weekends throughout the spring of 1961. Only four banders were named, Neil and Alice Kelley, W. Lamb, and John Roberts. The Long Point station was already taking a bite out of Point Pelee volunteers. In spite of this, 1,140 birds of 79 species were banded.[128]

The OBBA pulled out of Point Pelee completely in 1962 and concentrated on their new location at Long Point, where they re-established the Heliogland trap. Point Pelee was downgraded to a Bird Observatory, with banding done mainly for hawks and owls in the fall. Some results from 1959 to 1962 were reported in *Ontario Bird Banding*. During the period covered by this report, the banding station was in operation 141 days resulting in 9,179 birds of 133 species being banded, 24 foreign recoveries, (birds banded at Point Pelee and captured or otherwise found elsewhere) and 70 returns (the recapture of a bird at the same location after a period of 90 days). Statistics of note were, the large numbers of swallows banded in the spring only, and of hawks, almost all Sharp-shinned, banded in the fall only. There was also a much larger percentage of finches in the spring and thrushes in the fall. Returns were thought to be local breeding birds, with the interesting observation that the proportion of returns from migratory species such as Eastern Kingbird, Brown Thrasher, and Yellow Warbler were comparable with those of the non-migratory Northern Cardinal.[129]

In 1973, new Parks Canada regulations put a further crimp in the Point Pelee Observatory. Banding was only allowed provided it was being done as field work to support a particular study. Two such research projects were submitted and accepted: one a study of population dynamics of the Sharp-shinned Hawk migration at Point Pelee National Park and the other a study of Saw-whet Owl migration at Point Pelee National Park. This meant that banding was allowed only for these two species. All other birds trapped had to be released unbanded. Considering that these birds had already undergone the process of being trapped and handled, not banding them seemed irrational.

Daily notes written by the banders give a lively picture of the day-to-day struggles experienced by the Point Pelee Bird Observatory through its last year of activity. The banding station trailer was moved to the west side of the Tip, which was found to be a "most unfavourable" location by Jane Evans, the first bander there for the 1973 fall season. She felt that there was no privacy from visitors and that presented a problem many times, to the extent that operations had to cease temporarily as a consequence. She reports of days spent cleaning, repairing, and painting the trailer; of visitors who were "quite disgusted with the shameful way birds became entangled in nets"; and of a "well meaning lady [who] tried to take a 'poor' bird out of a 'fish net' and succeeded in strangling it."[130] Dennis Rupert, who was by this time in charge of Point Pelee banding, in his year end report, agreed with Evans. He pointed out the fact that operations were occasionally suspended on afternoons and holidays because of "interference and equipment damage caused by large crowds." Rupert then went on to describe a trailer sweltering in heat from direct sunlight, millions of biting Stable Flies, and stolen window screens—"cross-ventilation necessary to cool the trailer on hot days meant admitting hundreds of unwanted dinner guests through the screen-less windows."[131]

Coleman camping equipment was used for heat and light, and as if that were not enough, bander Ross Snider was a little perturbed when on October 16, 1973, the Tip washrooms were closed, "I guess we'll have to rough it for the rest of the week!"[132] With heat, crowds, flies, poor facilities, and vandalism, only one more adventure was needed to cover the gamut, and that one caught Bill Wasserfall unprepared on October 29: "The warden and the Mersea police came to get me off the point due to storm warnings of 8' [two and a half metre] waves ... couldn't get my car started so was towed up to the nature centre parking lot where I spent the night in the car."[133] In spite of all the frustrations, this turned out to be a good year in terms of coverage by the five banders and ten associates who worked forty-seven of the forty-nine days that had been scheduled.

One October night during that last year, Sarah Rupert, who still birdwatches and works at Point Pelee, stayed at the bird-banding trailer with her father while her mother and baby sister remained in Leamington. Not only was this an opportunity to have her father's attention and company, it also afforded her with a wonderful chance to see owls up close as they were brought in to be banded.

As this part of the Point Pelee birding history comes to an end, a statement by Marianne Gosztonyi Ainley in her book, *The Contribution of the Amateur to North American Ornithology: A Historical Perspective*, could serve as a eulogy for the banding station: "Bird banding emerged as one of the most important techniques in the study of the living bird. Amateurs participated in banding activities from the beginning and have aided significantly in bird migration projects and life history studies."[134]

Although Long Point banding operations evolved into Bird Studies Canada, an internationally respected institute with a budget of approximately $2.8 million, the banders who volunteered at Point Pelee laid the groundwork for banding in Ontario and deserve special recognition.

CHAPTER 6
Simplifying the Watching

On the desk at the Point Pelee National Park Visitor Centre sits a simple three-ringed binder. It was placed there in the mid-1970s and remains there to this day, beckoning the unwary. "The Book of Lies" as it is known—often with good reason—invites birders to fill its pages with interesting or rare sightings. Birders take their chances when writing in this book, and those new to the hobby are most likely to get caught innocently showing their ignorance by putting in something outrageous. Here the reason for the British birding maxim, "What's shot's history; what's seen's mystery," becomes clear.

Identification problems are part and parcel of birding, and even the most fantastic equipment cannot make up for carelessness or incompetence. In his book *Flashing Wings*, Richard M. Saunders writes of an occasion when he was birding with friends at Point Pelee in 1946. They met a party of members of the Detroit Audubon Society also enjoying an outing: "Among the Detroiters we met one woman who insisted on telling us that the Yellow-throats we saw and heard along the ditch were 'Hooded Warblers.' She got rather annoyed when we disagreed."[135] It is unlikely that better equipment would have made any difference to this lady; even holding the bird in her hand might not have convinced her. However, improvements in binoculars and telescopes have helped modern-day naturalists move more quickly from the realm of amateur to that of knowledgeable birder.

Binoculars and Spotting Scopes

Consider early scientists such as Alexander Wilson, who first tried a monocular glass or telescope in 1813; Audubon, who used one from time to time; and Henry Thoreau, who bought one in 1853 and used it frequently. These men were collectors and their reaction to a potential specimen was to shoot it first and see if they had a need for it later. Although telescopes were being used by sailors, soldiers, and astronomers, among others, the idea of using them to study birds would have seemed ludicrous to the naturalists who needed the skins to sell, to identify, or to prove a new record. After the US Civil War, the binocular began to replace the monocular (at two-power, often used as opera glasses). Field glass structure continued to improve with the first prism binoculars patented in France 1859 and four-powered glasses were being widely used by 1900.[136]

Quality of equipment is always a hot topic for discussion among birders, and the members of the Great Lakes Ornithological Club were no exception. Taverner owned two-power binoculars which he found to be inadequate. In a letter to Fleming, Taverner said: "I use a rather large pair of La Reine, Paris. However I am just negotiating with Wallace who can get the finest Zeise glasses I ever saw very cheap— $35.00—through friends from the old country."[137] In reply Fleming suggested that Taverner save his $35.00 and accept an excellent pair that he had but could not use. The goal of being able to identify birds through binoculars was important to Taverner, although he never left his .410 shotgun behind. The naturalists had no desire to kill every bird in sight. Fleming wrote wistfully of his desire, "just to watch the birds and record interesting things on the spot ... to be free of a gun and to have only glasses and a writing pad. I would get valuable material for habits and character."[138] But like many ornithologists of the time, he had no confidence in binoculars being able to produce accurate sight records.[139] Ludlow Griscom, noted ornithologist and writer as well as research curator of the Museum of Comparative Zoology, Harvard University, tells a story about such a diehard who was only convinced after he accompanied a group of young ornithologists into the field and shot each bird they identified by sight. Their sight identifications were correct, proving that "the field glass method was remarkably precise."[140]

Gradually, as binoculars and their reputation improved, birders trying to get a better look also became inventive. Bruce Falls, who went on to become a professor for the University of Toronto Department of Zoology, birding in the mid-1940s used "a badly scratched World War I gun sight ... and a telescope built out of one of his father's surveying instruments."[141] Fred Bodsworth, naturalist and writer, described his first binoculars and how he acquired them during the Great Depression: "I saved the labels off Libby pork and bean cans (I got most of them from garbage dumps, not from home) to acquire my first field glasses. When they came they were tiny four-power things, but I didn't recognize until much later how inadequate they really were. They were all I had for years, and when one lens dropped out and broke, I went on using them one-eyed for years more."[142]

Don and Barb Cavin began birding in 1958 and had to share binoculars: "The warblers were just pouring by us in the bush. We had one pair of binoculars between us and I couldn't get focused on any one of them."[143] Jean Kelly, a beginner birder in the 1980s, also had binocular problems: "I was working with an ancient and heavy pair of binoculars and found it really difficult to focus ... but I got hooked nevertheless."[144]

Homemade and old equipment such as this was a far cry from today's binoculars and 'scopes, which have simplified identification of gulls, ducks, geese, and shorebirds. At Point Pelee, with its acres of inaccessible marsh, one can set up a high-powered telescope on the tower at the Marsh Boardwalk and count swans and other waterfowl far out on Lake Pond. Also, the sandy spit at the end of Point Pelee can be quite long, making identification of resting gulls difficult, but Hamilton birder Kevin A. McLaughlin spends many hours viewing them through his 'scope. Being hearing impaired, he enjoys gulls, terns, and shorebirds, which allow him to rely more heavily on his observational skills. However, he does admit "without a doubt, the acquisition of my first spotting 'scope ... in October 1974, was a major stimulus for my interest in waterbirds."[145] A Red Knot—a bird which Swales and Taverner found at the Tip, shot, and brought back to camp in order to compare it with Coues' *Key to North American Birds*—can now be identified easily by today's birders with up-to-date equipment.

Bird Books

A timely reminder here might be this admonition by ornithologist Frank M. Chapman, "Let not the field student of today, who never knew the gun, forget that his glass has won its standing on a foundation which could have been laid only with the aid of the gun."[146] The shift to the use of binoculars and scopes was made possible by the excellent bird guides available, which in their turn were made possible by specimen collection. To recognize birds, one needs not only to see them, but also to have guidelines for their identification. Bird guides could not have been written without the collections of skins and plumages of each species, as well as specimens showing the plumages of individuals of each species at various ages. The book used by Taverner and Swales, Coues' *Key to North American Birds*, was the first manual that allowed anyone to identify a bird that they had never before seen. It was a set of two large books, published in 1872, in which birds were identified by colour, but there were no colour illustrations. One had to ferret out which bird one was seeing from the description. Colour illustrations gradually became part of bird guides, but as Fred Bodsworth points out, "*Colour Key to North American Birds* by Chapman and Reed, publication date 1903 (and there was very little colour in it)" was a "primitive" book. A slightly later book, *Birds of America*, published in 1917, had 106 paintings by Louis Agassiz Fuertes. The editorial staff and the advisory board for this publication included Lynds Jones, first professor of ornithology in the US, and read like a who's who of American birding. The trend toward bird guides with colour illustrations continued, making identification easier and encouraging amateur watchers.

Taverner's *Birds of Eastern Canada*, published in 1919, was another such book. It was so well received by the general public that a second edition was printed in 1921. The publication of this book was instrumental in making birdwatching a more accessible pastime. And it influenced young people such as George North, of Hamilton, Ontario, whose parents presented him with the book on his ninth birthday (January 1920), to take up the study of birds. North went on to become one of Hamilton's best-known ornithologists and a leading authority on birds in southern Ontario.[147] Not surprisingly, he also became a regular visitor to Point Pelee. Taverner went on to write *Birds of Western Canada* in 1926, and *Birds of Canada* in 1934.

These were excellent books, being specifically Canadian, and in all ways an improvement over those previously available. Nevertheless, an American was to make the great coup in bird books. Naturalist Roger Tory Peterson's *A Field Guide to the Birds*, published in 1934, literally revolutionized birding. The Peterson field guides became an instant success. Besides being small enough to carry in one's pocket, Peterson described specific markings that could be used for quick field identification of each bird, thereby opening the way for the casual birdwatcher. The Peterson method did have a few drawbacks, however. Tom Hince, former chief interpreter at Point Pelee National Park, points out that the "paint-by-numbers system really limits peoples' ability to look at birds. They don't look at the bird, they look at the field marks, so they don't notice tones, structure, posture and behaviour."[148] As good as binoculars had become, and as helpful as the field guides were, identification of birds that were of different species but looked alike was still a problem for beginners.

Recording Bird Songs

Many birders learned to identify bird sounds by spending a great deal of time in the field and paying close attention.

However, in 1954 people new to the sport were given an extra boost by virtue of the availability of bird song recordings. These were made possible through the efforts of ornithologist Dr. W. W. H. Gunn, who, in the course of his research on the birds of Point Pelee, made recordings of their songs.

His first recording, *Songs of Spring*, featured twenty-five species recorded in chronological order of spring arrival on side one. On side two, the same songs were grouped according to habitat, providing the listener with an opportunity to try out their skills.[149] A later recording included the "songs of 226 individual birds of 43 species of Fringillids of Eastern North America" and another covered the warblers. They were "highly recommended for all who would learn to recognize ... birds by ear as well as by sight."[150] The move from phonograph records, which were limited to indoor use, to tapes and portable tape players, enhanced the usefulness of the recordings. Today, computers allow birders to see and hear the bird at the same time, allowing them to make an audio-visual connection.

Three young birders from Holland were walking through Post Woods, May 1999. There were bird species here that they had never seen before, yet they could immediately name the bird making each call. Explaining this strange phenomenon to a naive Canadian, they said that they had listened to and memorized sound recordings of all birds that they might encounter on their trip to Point Pelee. Knowing the sound, they would follow it and find the bird more easily. This effort in preparation is certainly also an indication of how seriously some birders take their hobby. But keeping in mind that they will have spent a good deal of money on that one trip, one can understand their desire to be well-prepared and to avoid wasting time on a more common bird. Only the birds needed for their life lists would be pursued by these birders.

Transportation

Since Point Pelee is a good distance from large city centres, transportation has been a continuing challenge. Taverner spoke of taking the ferry across the Detroit River to Windsor, the train to Leamington, a horse and buggy to the east shore of Point Pelee, then on the return trip, walking from Point Pelee to Leamington through rain and clay, which stuck to boots and added pounds to already tired feet. Great Lakes Ornithological Club members travelled to Point Pelee at great physical cost to themselves, starting a tradition that would be followed by many other young ornithologists.

Don MacDonald, describing his 1941 visit, recalls taking the bus from Toronto to Chatham where he had already shipped his one-speed bicycle. He then biked from Chatham to Rondeau Provincial Park where he spent the night. The following day, he carried on to Point Pelee where he "spent the night on the concrete floor of the veranda of Post House." A few days later, John MacArthur and George North arrived. "They had bicycled from Toronto and Hamilton respectively!"[151]

For birders in the 1940s and 1950s, a sense of humour went a long way to overcoming the difficulties experienced at Point Pelee. Ron Tasker, making the trip with Bruce Falls in May 1946, stated, "I will never forget the 6+ hour drive in Bruce's father's car, almost driving off the Leamington dock into Lake Erie in the dark, camping out on a sand dune, which in the morning turned out to be covered by Prickly Pear Cactus, now long gone."[152]

Bristol Foster, who began birding here in 1948, when he was still in his teens, describes coming with others such as George Francis, Jim Woodford, and Don Burton: "We were short of money and we borrowed my father's car and paid him three cents a mile to use it. ... We always cooked and camped out on the beach. ... If there was rain we'd use some of the shelters. ... My new sleeping bag leaked feathers and I looked like I came out of a pillow fight in the morning. This always gave the others a good laugh."[153]

Fred Bodsworth made his first trip to Point Pelee in 1949 with William W. Smith of Toronto. They were driving out of Toronto when Smith remembered that he was supposed to have stopped at his bank to get money. In consternation, he turned to Bodsworth, who happily informed him, "Oh I've got lots of money, I've got 15 dollars!" To Bodsworth, fifteen dollars was a veritable fortune; certainly plenty of money to take to Point Pelee.[154]

Bob Curry drove from Hamilton, Ontario: "For several springs during the early 1960s, when I was at university, I would go to Pelee right after the final exam in early May. In 1964, ... I was with Dave Bissell. Our transportation was my very first car, a blue 1954 Chevrolet, which was nearing the end of its life. It gave new meaning to the phrase 'getting there is half the fun.' I called it, affectionately, 'The Indigo Wreck'."[155]

In sharp contrast to these stories, birdwatchers can now travel quickly and comfortably from anywhere in the world. British birder and photographer Peter A. Coe was able to catch a direct flight from London, England, to Detroit: a mere eleven- or twelve-hour trip. Coe, along with fellow photographer Dave Nichols, was staying at Sturgeon Woods Campground: "We didn't set off until 1:50 p.m. out

During May 2005, (left to right) Fred Bodsworth, Bruce Falls, John MacArthur, and Don MacDonald celebrated 65 years, although not necessarily consecutive, of birding at Point Pelee.

of the UK and we got here in time to set the tents up before it got dark. If we had set off in the morning we would have been here on time to set the tents up and go birding."[156]

Accommodation

Once birders arrived at Point Pelee, accommodations had to be found. Great Lakes Ornithological Club members had "Camp Coues," then The Shack. Some naturalists stayed with area residents but most just camped out, sometimes using a vacant building as shelter. In 1940, Don MacDonald with friends Ron Bremner, John A. Livingston, John MacArthur, and Bob Richie drove to Pelee for their first visit. They "camped at the south end of the road" where there was "a beat-up structure" which he believed to have

Aviation Inn was well liked by the birders. It was in business at Point Pelee National Park until 1961.

been the remains of the Life-saving Station.[157] Jim Woodford also mentions this structure, saying: "We used to sleep in the old boathouse at the end of the Point. If it was a nice night we just slept on the beach." [158] Bob Taylor described his first visit in 1953 at the age of thirteen, with several members of the Toronto Junior Naturalists and leader Ilmar Tavila. They arrived at Point Pelee, "long past midnight ... since it was raining we decided to camp in one of the picnic shelters ... some of us put our sleeping bags on the concrete floor while others slept precariously on top of the tables."[159] Bob Curry's descriptions highlight gradual changes in Point Pelee National Park policy:

> We would spread our sleeping bags on the tables and sleep. Well, we would attempt to sleep, but it usually meant about five hours of shivering in the fetal position. By dawn we

were just drifting off, when wealthier birders not long up from a warm night in a real bed woke us as they headed out to the Tip. Park officials frowned upon this practice, so we moved to the campgrounds to the north of the present-day Visitor Centre. There we would attempt the big sleep in the car. Now, I am slightly more than six feet tall, so attempting to survive a cold night in a car often resulted in paralysis for the first few hours of the day. So if it were really cold we would, after midnight, sneak into the campground laundry room and catch a few warm hours, hoping not to be banned from the Park.[160]

Alan Wormington, after hitchhiking the 300 kilometres from Hamilton, Ontario, to Point Pelee, chose to "spend the night undetected under a shelter along the Woodland Nature Trail."[161] Another Hamilton birder, Kevin McLaughlin, pulled into Point Pelee National Park for the first time in 1974. Not being aware of restrictions, he expected to camp in the Park. After spending a night in a motel and two nights tenting at Wheatley Provincial Park, he camped "on the lawn of one of the few remaining landowners at Point Pelee, a woman by the name of Mrs. Happy, who was renting grass space to birders for a few dollars per night."[162]

By this time, the space made available for camping at Point Pelee was limited, and designated for groups. Many birders twigged onto the idea of coming up with a phony name, such as Barry Griffiths' "The Barry Griffiths Bird Club," in order to camp with friends or family.[163] There was

Point Pelee Lodge (Post House) was located near the present day Sparrow Field.

also fun to be had in the campgrounds. Jim Coey remembers joining an impromptu band under one of the cooking shelters: "We collected a large crowd of people who were singing and dancing in the rain ... We were enjoying ourselves and fighting off the cold with the odd snort of Irish Whiskey when a shout from one of the tents informed us that some people were going to get up at five to watch birds. Imagine!"[164] Today, camping is still popular amongst birders, although the policy regulating camping in the Park is strictly enforced.

Not all birders liked camping or were impecunious youngsters, and the amenities of home were available at places such as the Aviation Inn and Point Pelee Lodge. Aviation Inn, originally the home of the Girardin family, was situated slightly north of where today's Visitor Centre is located. In 1922, Bert Girardin (or Gardiner, as he was known to the birders) sold the house and surrounding land, which included the GLOC "Shack," to Oscar Richards of Detroit, who added the shack to the original building and started a restaurant he called Aviation Inn. In 1939, Helen McCormick Wolfe bought, repaired, and reopened the Inn. Here older and more established birders would stay the night. It was particularly favoured by those from Toronto, such as James Baillie and Dr. William Gunn.

Richard M. Saunders, during a visit May 1946, was pleased and surprised that the Aviation Inn could accommodate him and his friends at the last minute. He also described breakfast as "a superb meal like all meals at Aviation Inn."[165]

Don and Barb Cavin remember Aviation Inn, 1958: "We arrived late at night ... every room was full except the one that was usually reserved for the cook, so we got to sleep in the cook's room above the kitchen. One thing we liked ... and still remember, is the civilized way they served the meals. They had white linen table cloths, silverware, little pots of jam and ... butter, brown sugar and cream for your porridge—it was wonderful."[166]

In the mid fifties, Bob Taylor and fellow bird bander Doug Dow appreciated the hospitality found at the Aviation Inn when they were invited to supper by the owner, Mrs. Wolfe. "She probably found out that we were living on junk food and the free samples that we got from tours of the Heinz plant in Leamington."[167]

Point Pelee Lodge was situated near the present day Sparrow Field and much further south on the Point than Aviation Inn. Post House, as it was originally known, was a large cement-block house that was bought by Point Pelee National Park in 1938 and refurbished the following year. It had a checkered service history, having been a family home, rented out, unoccupied, and used by bird researchers in the early 1940s. Finally the building was licensed by the Park to Mr. Arthur Reissner who ran it as Point Pelee Lodge. Bird banders were familiar with the lodge. Bob Taylor recalls its "dinners, especially the pies ... are not to be forgotten as we sat around a huge round table swapping tales with other birders in the late fifties."[168] Like Aviation Inn, birders filled the rooms during May. But unlike the Inn, the birders who stayed at the Lodge generally came from Buffalo rather than Toronto. This situation made for some good-natured rivalry between the temporary occupants of the two buildings.

That fun all came to an end in 1961, when Aviation Inn was removed in order to accommodate the present day Visitor Centre. By that time Point Pelee Lodge was being used for staff housing, and birders looking for comfortable lodgings had no alternative within Park gates. Bill Martin remembers that by then Wigle's Motel on Talbot Street East in Leamington had become a birder-friendly place to stay. Run by Doris Wigle, it was a hub for the "favoured old-timers." Here again they found a cordial welcome, a personal touch, and excellent cooking, which included "many home-made preserves ... set out on the tables for all to enjoy."[169] The late 1960s and early 1970s brought another group of young birders to Point Pelee: those who wanted to sleep in a bed at night but were unable or unwilling to pay a great deal to do so. Tom Hince remembered the not-so-comfortable, inexpensive accommodations provided by the Lakeshore Motel:

> It is legendary among that particular core of birders because it was dirt cheap accommoda-

tions and it was where Mike Malone's Pelee Wings store is now. There were about seven to eight units and it was run by a gentleman by the name of Mr. Costa who was in his 80s and rather unstable. We'd have great parties in our rooms and we'd end up paying our rent in beer cases—he'd back his pickup truck up to the door and we'd load all our empty beer cases and then he'd want a few more dollars. We were never quite sure how much the room was going to cost. We'd hand him a five and he'd sort of gesture with his hands a little bit more—we'd give him a few more dollars.[170]

That description paints a picture of a place that is a far cry from motels of today. Pelee Days Inn, one of the more lavish accommodations nearby, boasts of an indoor pool but is better known by birders for its access to the west side of Sturgeon Creek. Management has allowed and even encouraged birding behind its premises, no doubt reaping the benefits of this lenience. Birders, in turn, have seen excellent birds there, including a White-faced Ibis, a new species for the area, in May 2003.[171]

All About The Birds

Gilbert White was a British naturalist and clergyman whose letters to fellow naturalists were published in 1789, in a book called *The Natural History of Selborne*. This book went through many reprints and was an inspiration to aspiring naturalists. Known as the patron saint of the amateur naturalist, White wrote, "all nature is so full, that that district produces the greatest variety which is the most examined."[172] At Pelee in early May, many eyes bring forth the unexpected, but as bird columnist Peter Whalen points out, rarities might go virtually unnoticed in late May and early June:

> In a parking lot at Point Pelee National Park on Monday, a lone birder stood pointing at the sky and shouting, "Mississippi Kite! Mississippi Kite!" It was a sign of the times that all 22 tourists in the lot stared at the odd performance and maybe edged away. All but a few birders of spring had gone home; the Mississippi Kite floated off on grey wings, a rarity that would have started an instant celebration a week earlier. Once again Point Pelee has put on a late-May show that birders of early May never see. On Sunday, a Sharp-tailed Sparrow played to a sparse binoculared audience near the tip of the point. On Saturday, the frequently misidentified Blue Grosbeak performed.[173]

Obviously birders must be at Point Pelee in order to record Point Pelee birds, a fact which is reflected in the numbers. Taverner and Swales included a total of 209 species in their 1907-1908 annotated list of birds of Point Pelee. While the members of the GLOC continued to visit Point Pelee annually new species were frequently added to the list. However, from the early 1920s to early 1940s Point Pelee did not receive heavy visitation by active birders; consequently few new species were recorded. The first official checklist of birds for Point Pelee, at least in booklet form, was not published until 1960, when 288 species were included. Subsequent editions list 315 species in 1968; 336 in 1975; 349 in 1989; 362 in 1997; and finally 370 in 2000. Various adjustments have been made along the way. Some species have been deleted due to inadequate documentation. Also, taxonomic changes, "splits" and "lumps," have altered the totals. Currently the total number of birds recorded at Point Pelee stands at 383 species; the two most recent additions are Slaty-backed Gull and Ivory Gull, both of which were found in January 2006.[174]

Point Pelee remains arguably the best location in Ontario to observe migrating birds. To date, more species have been recorded at Point Pelee than any other location in Ontario, with the exception of just two—Toronto and Hamilton. However, the official Point Pelee Birding Area is just a 24 kilometre diameter circle, whereas the designated areas of these two other locations are far larger.

Among the changes that have taken place since the Great Lakes Ornithological Club members visited Point Pelee, possibly the most significant is the amount of money being spent by birders on their hobby. Fred Bodsworth remarks: "Some of my sharpest memories of those early years as a burgeoning naturalist were how I had to make do with few of the aids that create virtually overnight naturalists today. ... Under these conditions, it took me five years to gain the expertise that today's beginning naturalists get in their first year."[175]

CHAPTER 7
Turning Points

There were sixteen of them crammed into one room of the Lakeshore Motel. Space was at a premium, but the price was right and they weren't concerned about comfort. They were ambitious, energetic, egotistical hotshots. They were young and talented. They were here to see all the birds that Point Pelee had to offer. Tonight they might relax, have a few drinks, get into a fight, but tomorrow they would shine. Birding was their passion and they lived it passionately. It was early in the 1970s and these young men and others like them had turned birding on its ear.

Point Pelee had served as an informal ornithological education centre for many a young birder, beginning with Taverner and Swales in the first decade of the twentieth century. For them, study meant shooting and skinning. Their books were limited as were their binoculars. Then came William Gunn's study of reverse migration in the 1940s, which involved an organized series of "watches." Gunn was following the academic path, by this time both possible and desirable for serious ornithologists. A decade later, bird banding was initiated by five members of the Toronto Intermediate Naturalists who depended on their elders for mentoring, permission, and financial support.

Another fifteen years saw birding move into the fast lane when the tail end of the baby boom produced a whole new set of young birders. They depended on adults only as long as they had to, quickly acquiring licences to drive, and money of their own to spend. Better guides and equipment far beyond that with which the older birders had worked were available. They answered to no one, and respected only those who were capable of keeping up with their hectic pace.

Ornithology as a science had evolved from amateurs working in the field and learning as they went, to a practice of accredited professionals. This change was fuelled by the provincial and federal governments' need for naturalists to staff museums, parks, and conservation areas, enforce conservation measures such as the Migratory Birds Convention Act, and teach in universities and colleges. The fact that many ornithologists were now government employees meant that in Ontario, Ottawa, and Toronto became focal points for the birding community. Increasingly, these professional ornithologists came to Point Pelee for what it could deliver—rare birds and birds in migration. They had little interest in further study of the area, and "into this ... zone where less was being done by "professional" ornithologists in such fields as distribution, seasonality, ecology, and even migration, the birders came."[176] As birder numbers increased and birding was taken up casually or on an intermittent basis, the quality of birder was of concern to many established birders, both amateur and professional. Simultaneously, and probably a by-product of this concern, a rift developed between amateur and professional ornithologists. M.T. Myres points this out in a 1963 article published in the *Ontario Naturalist*: "I am a firm believer in the mutual advantages to be obtained both by amateurs and by professionals from good relationships between them, a relationship which is in sad shape in much of Canada."[177] The situation in Ontario was no exception, demonstrated by the fact that by this time birders had already begun to divide themselves into two camps, behind such leaders as the professional, James Baillie, from the Royal Ontario Museum in Toronto, or the amateur, George North, birder from Hamilton. Like Baillie in Toronto, North had a tremendous influence on many young Hamilton birders who were "spread across the country."[178] John MacArthur remembers birding with North and was amazed by his ability:

> When I knew him, he could identify birds that the rest of us could barely see, so one day I looked through his binoculars to see how he did it and found that they were only useable on one side—the other being completely smashed inside. Remarkable! He did with one eye what the rest of us could not do with two. The only explanation I can come up with is excellent eyesight and endless practice.[179]

There was no argument about North's competence. Why then was there such an obvious split between the two factions that many birders took note of it? Was the competition between the two men? Between the professional and the amateur field observer? Between the followers themselves? Or between the two cities?

Gerry Bennett, member of the TOC and editor of *Birdfinding in Canada*, describes an incident in his journal from 1953 in which snobbery and complacency among the established birders worked to everyone's detriment:

> All over the Point today, reports of rarities were being turned in. I was sitting at the Federation [FON] booth at the tip talking to Bill Gunn and Lucie McDougall when a young fellow reported a Harris's Sparrow and I am ashamed to say that I didn't believe him and my skepticism resulted in my losing probably the best chance I will ever have of seeing this bird as the record proved perfectly sound and several observers saw the bird.[180]

The same kind of reaction was observed by Bob Curry when he and Dave Bissell reported a Chuck-will's-widow:

> In the pre-dawn of May 11, 1964, I sat abruptly up in my sleeping bag. A loud rippling song from the area of the road on the east side of the campgrounds instantly awoke me. By the third song I realized it was a Chuck-will's-widow! Now, I knew it was on the Ontario checklist from an old, odd record at Pelee but I also knew that this was only the second for the province.[181] Of course, it was a 'lifer' for us. So we staggered out to the road and listened to the "Chuck." Occasionally it would stop singing and we would see a large, shadowy form coursing up and down the road. As it got lighter, the singing stopped.
>
> Excitedly, we went out to the Tip to tell people. Now, in 1964 there were not hordes at

Pelee in May but we still were able to tell about 50 or more birders of our good fortune. We added that surely the bird had gone to roost and that those on the spot at sunset had a great chance of hearing and seeing it again.

When evening came we were there but only a couple of other cars joined us. All we could think was that the two young upstarts had little credibility. So we quite gloated when, on cue, the Chuck-will's-widow started up. It only sang for a few minutes and I don't recall that we saw it that evening. However, we were pleased, in a perverse way, to see a line of about 20 cars parked alongside the road for the next day or two, listening for the now "confirmed" but long-gone Chuck-will's-widow.[182]

There is a decade between the two incidents described above, but in both cases the young birders were beginning to outpace those who thought that they knew Point Pelee best, and they were not necessarily coming from the halls of higher learning. It is a certainty that the huge increase in birdwatchers during the 1960s and 1970s was not matched by an equally large increase in the numbers taking up ornithology as a profession. Birders were coming from all walks of life—they were accountants, ministers, housewives, and more. They were becoming increasingly competent, many were self-taught, and they were increasingly involved in rare-bird records committees, breeding bird surveys, atlases, Christmas Bird Counts, and hawk watches. That twelve per cent of all papers published in ornithological journals in North America in 1975 were written by amateurs,[183] at a time when journals in other scientific fields had ceased to publish non-professional articles, showed that they would not easily be marginalized by academics. The fact that there were now so many people involved also made it more difficult for the professionals to keep abreast of all the new data without help. Meanwhile serious amateur field observers began to feel dissatisfied with what they could accomplish working alone, and local nature clubs could not always meet their needs.

Also, birding was shifting into high gear in the early to mid 1970s with youngsters such as Alan Wormington, Tom Hince, Michael Runtz, Donald A. Sutherland, Mike Bentley, Ron Ridout, Bruce D. Mactavish, and Bruce M. Di Labio trekking to Point Pelee. The "Peanut Butter Brigade"—as Peter Whalen, writer of a bird column for the *Globe and Mail*, would call them—reported higher numbers and more rare birds than previously seen, and initially their integrity was questioned.

One of these young men would eventually figure heavily in Point Pelee National Park history: Tom Hince from Ottawa. He was a thirteen-year-old with an ambition to travel to Pelee to see all the birds that he couldn't see back home. His mother had given him *Birds of Canada* by Earl Godfrey, and in it he read about Yellow-breasted Chat and Prothonotary Warbler—both birds seen at Point Pelee. Hitching a ride with Vi Humphries, administrative assistant to Earl Godfrey and an active member of The Ottawa Field-Naturalists' Club, Hince skipped school for a week in May 1971 to attend the do-it-yourself educational birding centre that was Point Pelee. On the way Humphries got lost. They ended up at Hillman Marsh Conservation Area (then known as Stein's Marsh) where they saw a flock of twenty-eight Glossy Ibis come in to land. As they watched, fifteen Cattle

Egret flew in and landed next to them. Once in Point Pelee National Park, Hince discovered a Kentucky Warbler on the Woodland Nature Trail. Only Peter Whalen, birding there with some friends, believed him, and with Whalen's encouragement, Hince relocated the bird.

Another newcomer was Alan Wormington, whose grandmother had been a biology teacher and owned a cottage in Haliburton. At the cottage Wormington would spend summer days looking at butterflies, birds, and moths. His family lived in Hamilton where he spent a great deal of his time wandering about the woods and fields of Dundas Marsh. One day his older sister came home from high school and said that her biology teacher travelled to places such as Point Pelee and Long Point and kept notes of all the birds that he saw. Wormington, deciding that he could do the same, started keeping notes on November 1, 1967. That month his mother bought a *Peterson's Field Guide to the Birds* and the *Golden Guide to Birds of North America* for him for Christmas. Wormington found out that the Hamilton Christmas Bird Count was going to be held before Christmas, and he knew that his mother had bought the books he needed. Rather than argue with her stubborn thirteen-year-old, his mother opted for giving him an early Christmas in the form of the two bird guides.

One of Wormington's first visits to Point Pelee was in May 1969, with his father. He was looking for moths at the Visitor Centre around midnight when he heard a Chuck-will's-widow singing from the direction of Tilden's Woods. It was only the third record for Point Pelee. Wormington would find many more rarities at Point Pelee during the following decades. In fact, as of 2006 he has been responsible for the addition of 22 species to the *Point Pelee Checklist*

Pictured here with Alan Wormington, Roger Tory Peterson visits Point Pelee, May 1982.

of Birds. One of his most important records was the addition of Lesser Nighthawk to the Canadian list on April 29, 1974. It was 7:00 p.m. and he was driving by the Marsh Boardwalk parking lot on the way to his dollar-a-night campsite at Mrs. Happy's cottage when he saw what he thought was a Common Nighthawk. Then he noticed the bird had buff wing patches rather than the expected white, "Since the bird was obviously something exotic, I immediately grabbed my camera and was able to take 13 photographs in quick succession as the bird circled overhead. I then put my camera down and—incredibly—the bird had disappeared, never to be seen again."[184] The photographs were sent to Earl Godfrey of the National Museum of Natural Sciences in Ottawa, who concluded, "the evidence is that this bird was a Lesser Nighthawk female."[185] With this confirmation in hand, the Ontario Ornithological Records Committee

(OORC) accepted the report and to this day it is the only record of Lesser Nighthawk for all of Ontario and for the Great Lakes Region. Had Wormington not provided a picture, this record would probably not exist.

A member of the OORC, Clive E. Goodwin, writer and ornithologist, was known to look at the reports of the young birders with a jaundiced eye: "Often young birders [are] on the emotional highs that big days at Pelee can produce, and often [go] long periods with neither rest nor adequate meals. These conditions can lead to all kinds of mistakes, overestimates and wild rumours."[186] He was among a cadre of older birders who were unable to accept that youth could outdo experience and that field skills could also come from a natural ability to see the whole bird—its "jizz." According to British birder Mark Cocker, "Jizz is an arcane but much-bandied term in birding parlance ... it now refers to each separate bird's indefinable, almost inarticulable visual 'personality.'"[187] Along with their natural talent, these youths were single-minded in their pursuit of birds and spent a great deal of their time in the field, both in their own areas and on trips to Point Pelee. Hince and his birding friends in Ottawa saved their money to go on a birding trip every other weekend. Wormington made fifty-two visits to Point Pelee before he began working there in 1978. There is no doubt that their hard work played a large part in their success. Nevertheless, a generation gap of monumental proportions was growing and Point Pelee was in the thick of it.

Maybe there was good reason to be skeptical about reports of rare bird sightings. Misidentification in the field was not unheard of and ornithologists no longer had the dead bird to examine. Something had to replace specimens for the purpose of record keeping and scientific bird study. Myres was already calling for a system for the confirmation of rare bird records in 1963, remarking: "Ontario seems to have a rather sordid reputation in regard to rarities." He goes on to suggest that birders in this province should consider setting up a rarities committee much like the one already in place in Britain where it is "a point of honour that ... they must submit detailed notes, written in the field, in substantiation of their record."[188]

There was no question that such a setup was necessary or that it would have an impact on Point Pelee where rarities were known to show up with some regularity. In 1970, the Ontario Ornithological Records Committee (OORC) was established to review rare bird sightings for provincial records. This committee would, "take a written account of an observation and assess that account against the available information on identifying the species in question in the field. If the account seemed fully convincing, the report would be accepted for publication, but if the information supplied did not clearly eliminate some other species as a possibility it would probably be rejected."[189]

Goodwin, who wrote the Ontario seasonal summary for *Audubon Field Notes* (later *American Birds*), was the motivating force behind the establishment of the OORC. He and his regional writers had to decide which observations made by other people were credible, and there were no specific guidelines for doing this. He wanted to introduce a systematic way of accepting or rejecting bird sightings. Members on the OORC were David Brewer, representing the OBBA, George Peck, Charles Long, and later, Ross James, representing the ROM, and a less active representative from the *Ontario Field Biologist*. The meetings were held at the ROM or at Goodwin's home. Although, Goodwin felt that there should be a change of delegates on the committee; it was difficult to get anyone to accept a position. As it was, even with the advent of the OORC, Goodwin, because he had a deadline to consider, had to decide what went into the Ontario seasonal summary. This put him in a position where he had control over what sightings were included, and he inadvertently angered many birders whose records were discarded. Although the establishment of the Ontario Ornithological Records Committee was a step in the right direction, it did not help Goodwin in the way that he had hoped. Also, with all the members of the OORC being representatives of specific organizations such as the OBBA, the *Ontario Field Biologist*, and the Royal Ontario Museum, this meant that the decision makers were all professionals who spent less time in the field, while those being judged were amateurs with no voice. There was no structure for accountability, and, for the time being, amateur field observers were frustrated into silence.

Meanwhile, the OORC encouraged the establishment of regional records committees. The Point Pelee Rare Bird Record Committee was set up in 1976. Some of the people involved were Rob Watt, who represented the Park (chairman), Paul D. Pratt, Joseph P. Kleiman, Dennis Rupert, James W. Wilson Sr., and Keith J. Burk. These were just the first members—there were others who later worked on this committee—all had two things in common; they were reliable birders and interested in Point Pelee.

With bird records scattered, an outdated checklist, and no seasonal status explaining which species of bird could be found at Point Pelee, the Point Pelee Rare Bird Record Committee members felt that there was a need for the Park to hire someone who was competent to deal with May birding issues. Accordingly, in 1978 and again in 1979, Alan Wormington was hired as the expert birder for the month of May. In 1980 the Park added him to their staff as an interpreter, a full-time seasonal position. He systematically organized all the Point Pelee bird records in order to better serve the birding public and provide intelligent answers to their questions. Wormington discovered that Dr. George Stirrett had collected all bird observations, literature, and records for Point Pelee, up to and including the 1970s, and had the information written on species index cards. These were with Stirrett in New Brunswick, but Wormington felt that the Stirrett files should be kept at Point Pelee where they were needed. Stirrett agreed, and Wormington flew to New Brunswick where he packaged up the files for shipment back to Point Pelee. Back at the Park, he organized the Stirrett files as part of his work, and he also took on the responsibility of compiling birding data.

It was not all work for Alan; it was an opportunity to be where he wanted to be. For example, on September 3, 1980, he and Ron Ridout did a "Big Sit," an activity engaged in all around North America, similar to a Big Day or Big Year, but the object is to sit in one spot all day and record birds. They were perched on top of a small building at the Tip of Point Pelee from 6:00 a.m. until 8:45 p.m. with mosquitoes eating them early in the morning, Stable Flies biting all day, and a cloudless 30 degrees Celsius to contend with. The bird total was exactly one hundred species; 9,000 Barn Swallows and 317 Cliff Swallows were the most notable high counts. Wormington stated that "September 3 happened to be a Barn Swallow day ... high numbers [were] the most interesting and important" finding of that Big Sit.[190] Although the

Alan Wormington and Ron Ridout spend fifteen hours watching birds from the top of a building at the Tip of Point Pelee, September 3, 1980.

Big Sit was not repeated, it is a common practice with many birders to spend the morning hours at the Tip watching and recording migrating birds.

In 1981, after going through all available records, Wormington put together the first edition of the *Point Pelee National Park Seasonal Status of Birds*. Prior to that, in the winter of 1979-80, he wrote his first seasonal summary of Point Pelee for *American Birds*—the winter summary—and sent it to Clive Goodwin. Until that time, Alice Kelley, an associate of the Cranbrook Institute of Science (Bloomfield Hills, Michigan), had been the *American Birds* compiler for all Ontario records from Essex, Kent, and Lambton counties as well as those from her own area. Wormington sent his records directly to Goodwin. Since he had already compiled them, he felt that going through Kelley was an unnecessary extra step. He also argued that Point Pelee should be considered a separate sub-region. And he was concerned that Point Pelee records were not otherwise being submitted reliably to Kelley, who by this time was not a regular birder at the Point. Goodwin argued that Kelley had adequately covered the area until then, but Wormington insisted that not all records were getting to Goodwin or at least not getting to *American Birds*.

By this time Wormington and other field observers were taking issue with the OORC over the fact that too many reliable rare bird reports were not being accepted, and as a result many field observers were no longer sending in their sightings. They saw a decided "Toronto area bias"[191] in the seasonal summaries in *American Birds*, and some well-documented sightings were not being included in records for the province. Subsequently, a meeting was held January 1982 at the Federation of Ontario Naturalists' headquarters in Toronto,

> To consider a restructuring of the provincial records committee. From that meeting a new Ontario Bird Records Committee emerged, with a plan of operation similar to those in various other parts of the world. ... The membership of the initial OBRC was selected from those assembled in January 1982 and they were charged with drawing up a constitution for the committee, of designating a subcommittee to form the Ontario Field Ornithologists (OFO) group, adjudicating the reports received during the year. The present OBRC consists of six members plus a secretary. Two members will

retire each year and be replaced from among
the members of OFO. The secretary is elected
annually. ... The present OBRC membership
includes R. Curry (Chairman), R. James (secretary), A.D. Brewer, T. Hince, P.D. Pratt, D.A.
Sutherland and A. Wormington.[192]

The Ontario Field Ornithologists had yet to be organized
in January 1982, but it was understood by the people at that
original meeting that such an organization would be founded,
and that the new OBRC would be a committee of the OFO
and answerable to its membership. It is obvious, since the
meeting took place in their building, that it had the support
of the FON, and the decisions that were made there to
restructure the bird records committee were to the satisfac-
tion of all concerned, including the members of the OORC.

Four months later, a "small group of birders from around
the province sat down one night at Point Pelee to discuss
the possibilities of an organization dedicated to the study of
the birdlife of Ontario. The various pros and cons of such a
group were volleyed back and forth, along with possible
aims and purposes, late into the evening."[193] An inaugural
meeting took place November 13, 1982, at Aldershot High
School in Burlington where an "enthusiastic group of about
125 people endorsed in principle the formation of the
Ontario Field Ornithologists."[194] On the OFO Board were
Ron Ridout (president), Bill Crins (vice-president), Verne
Evans (treasurer), Doug McRae (secretary), Don Fraser
(membership secretary), Chip and Linda Weseloh (editors),
Don Sutherland (Ontario Bird Records Committee representative), and Mike Runtz and Sarah Wood (directors). It
was also decided that OFO would publish a journal called

Ontario Birds: "The journal will ... provide a forum for the exchange and dissemination of ideas and knowledge among Ontario field ornithologists." The first publication was set for April 1983 and a Pelee weekend meeting was planned for May 14 and 15 of that year. The OFO planned to hold field meetings at Point Pelee in May and offer birding hikes, but that was short living, possibly due to the overcrowding at Point Pelee in May. However, trips to the area have since taken place during fall migration. The organization also supplied the structure so badly needed for serious Ontario birders. and now has an established track record of over twenty-one years. Since its inception, the OFO has published a journal (*Ontario Birds*) and in later years a newsletter (*OFO News*) was added. More recently they have developed a listserv and a website, ONTBIRDS, which allows birders across the province to share their sightings. Serious birding in Ontario was no longer exclusive to professionals; an environment had been created where all serious birders have equal standing. The OFO presidents over the years have also included women such as Gerry Shemilt, Margaret Bain, and Jean Iron, who was president for an unprecedented nine years, from 1995 to 2004.

With the OBRC and OFO stars rising, other changes began to take place as well. In March 1982, after eighteen years of volunteering his time to write the *Ontario Seasonal Summary Reports for American Birds*, Goodwin was relieved to hand the reins to Dr. Ron Weir, a leading birder from Kingston.[195] Weir informed birders that there was no "official connection between *American Birds* and the OBRC."[196] He went on to explain that if the material sent to him needed OBRC documentation, then the observer should send a separate submission to them. Weir was working

Jean Iron, president of the Ontario Field Ornithologists from 1995 to 2004 at the Tip of Point Pelee, May 2005.

under the same conditions as Goodwin had before him; the seasonal summary to *American Birds* was time sensitive, and could not wait for the OBRC decision-making process, which could take up to a year. Therefore, Weir would include all sightings of interest. Also, in spite of Wormington's desire to have Point Pelee made a sub-region, it was still included in the sub-region Lambton, Kent, and Essex, for which Alice Kelley was still cited as sub-regional editor. It was not until 1984 that Wormington was named sub-regional editor for the Point Pelee Birding Area.[197] In that capacity, Wormington continues to send in Point Pelee records, twenty-four years after he began. He also sent the records to *Birders Journal* during its publication, from 1991 to 2004 inclusive.

Even though members of the "Peanut Butter Brigade" were now in positions of importance, both in Ontario birding organizations and Point Pelee National Park, all did not run smoothly. As a member of both the Ontario Bird Records Committee and seasonal staff at Point Pelee National Park, Wormington made sure that all the old rare bird reports from Point Pelee got to the OBRC. This had the OBRC dealing with dozens of written reports that had never been reviewed before. Besides that, the OBRC began to reassess some decisions made by the OORC, and planned to revise the *Ontario Checklist of Birds* to reflect any changes. The committee informed birders that "continual changes to the checklist are possibly forthcoming as the OBRC reviews the status of every species in Ontario."[198] Not everyone on the committee was happy about taking this on. Hince felt that the old records were part of history and should be preserved as such. He suggested that any researcher could accept or reject the old sightings as they saw fit, and it was not the job of the OBRC to review these. On that point, Hince ended up resigning from the committee. Indirectly the activities of the OBRC also brought to an end the Point Pelee Rare Bird Records Committee. Because all Ontario records would be dealt with by the OBRC, and since Wormington sent Point Pelee's seasonal reports to the Ontario compiler for *American Birds* long before the Pelee committee had a chance to meet, it was thought that there would be little if anything left for it to do, so it was deemed redundant in 1985.

There were changes at Point Pelee as well when Wormington was joined on staff by Mike Runtz and Tom Hince in 1983. The "Peanut Butter Brigade" now had to learn to deal with internal squabbling, government planning, and red tape. But this didn't last long: Wormington left in 1985, and Mike Runtz was only there for a couple of

seasons, leaving Hince as the only member of the "Peanut
Butter Brigade" on staff. Peter Whalen succinctly addresses
this situation in a *Globe and Mail* column, May 1, 1985:
"Point Pelee birding will be a little tougher. Traditional
morning bird hikes led by a park naturalist and popular with
new birders have been canceled—a small part of the
Environment Ministry's cost cutting campaign. And bird
experts among the park naturalists have fallen to one this
spring from three last year. ... but apparently [this] results
from two late resignations. "[199]

Of those "hotshots" coming to Point Pelee in the 1970s,
Mike Runtz has taught a natural history course at Carleton
University for some time now, has become a well-known
author and wildlife photographer, and has a half-hour television show, *Wild By Nature*, on the Life Network. Ron
Ridout made a career for himself working at the Long Point
Bird Observatory, which later became Bird Studies Canada,
in Port Rowan. Bruce Di Labio lives in Ottawa where he
teaches birding and leads birding tours. Don Sutherland is a
zoologist working for the Ministry of Natural Resources at
the Natural Heritage Information Centre in Peterborough.
Bruce Mactavish lives in St. John's, Newfoundland, where
he works for LGL Ltd., which specializes in environmental
assessment surveys. Hince now does stock footage for video
and television productions, contracts birding studies for
regional governments, and leads his own tours to destina-
tions as diverse as Texas, Australia, South Africa, and
Venezuela. Pratt took a position with the City of Windsor at
Ojibway Park. Wormington worked seasonally at Point
Pelee with Parks Canada for several years, and also eleven
years at the MNR's Fisheries Research Station at nearby
Wheatley Harbour. Currently he is a consulting biologist

and has worked on dozens of environmental projects across southern Ontario, in addition to the Yukon, Hudson Bay and the Gulf of Mexico. He also leads birding tours to various locations, including Point Pelee. These are just some of the many new young birders who started coming to Point Pelee in the early 1970s, and all of them continue to be aggressive birders.

In 1989 a team of two Canadians, Paul Pratt and Tom Hince, along with Michael E. Carlson of Michigan, entered the World Series of Birding in New Jersey, a twenty-four-hour contest based at Cape May. The team won fourth place, spotting 195 of the 201 species found by all participants.[200] Since that time, with various combinations of members—Glenn A. Gervais acted as driver for several years and Bruce Di Labio replaced Mike Carlson—this team has entered the New Jersey World Series of Birding, the Great Texas Birding Classic, and the Space Coast Challenge in Florida. In 1997 they won first place in the New Jersey World Series, ahead of fifty-six other teams. This was their third first place trophy since they began entering the event in 1989.[201] In the Great Texas Birding Classic they broke a twenty-three-year-old Texas record for a Big Day marathon in 2001. Tom Hince, Paul Pratt, Bruce Di Labio, and driver, Ethan J. Meleg, identified 233 species—two more than the record—during a twenty-four-hour period covering a 1,300-kilometre trek.[202] On June 2, 2006, Hince and Pratt did a Big Day in Manitoba and "broke the long standing all time Canadian big day record (which had been set in Manitoba 1987). The old record was 205 species and we managed to find 212!"[203]

As for Alan Wormington, in 1999 and 2000, he was doing migration research for Louisiana State University on an oil platform in the Gulf of Mexico. In 2001 he was chosen as one of a team of six American, Canadian, and Dutch ornithologists, habitat specialists and technicians sponsored by Carl Zeiss Sports Optics to search Louisiana's Pearl River Wildlife Management Area for the Ivory-billed Woodpecker. On April 1, 2000, a forestry student hunting there was taken seriously when he described what he believed to be a pair of Ivory-billed Woodpeckers, a bird thought to be extinct, and of which there have been no confirmed sightings for upwards of fifty years. J. Van Remsen, the ornithologist with Louisiana State University who hand-picked the team, said of Wormington: "The number of amazing birds that he has found through the years is remarkable. His name has international recognition among birders in terms of field experience."[204] Wormington and his colleagues started out in January 2002 on a month-long search which resulted in several interesting finds and possible indicators that the Ivory-billed Woodpecker still exists. Unfortunately, there was no actual sighting of the bird.

In 2005 Wormington decided to do a "Big Year" in the Point Pelee Birding Area. He finished the year with a remarkable 292 species (ninety-seven per cent) of the 301 total recorded by all observers that year. It was a fantastic year for both him and Point Pelee. Wormington, who has been keeping statistics since 1979, pointed out that "prior to 2005 ... the difference between the highest and lowest years dating back to 1979 was only 18 species—a relatively narrow range. However, with the inclusion of 2005 the high/low range jumps to 30 species, a significant increase of 12. ... The number of species recorded in 2005 alone is equal to all species found at Point Pelee from 1877 to about the year

1964—a span of 87 years!"[205]

Wormington holds the record for the most bird species seen at Point Pelee with 357, and in Ontario he also leads the birding statistics with 431 species on his provincial list.

In their capacities as leaders and educators these birders have had many opportunities to influence others. One example is Michael A. Biro who, at seventeen years of age, found a Bullock's Oriole in his backyard in Toronto. The date was April 1, 1980. Biro called FON headquarters, was told to call Goodwin who, with birding companion Harry Kerr, came to confirm the oriole ID, and the word went out over the Birding Hotline. The oriole stayed in the vicinity for several days, bringing Biro into contact with many birders, including Paul Pratt, who came to see it. The meeting with Pratt encouraged Biro to begin making the spring trip to Point Pelee. He soon began guiding and by May 2004 celebrated twenty-five years of leading tours to Point Pelee.

There are undoubtedly birders who visit Point Pelee for whom the OBRC is just so much politics, who do not have an interest in organizations, and who do not care about bird statistics. These people simply enjoy birding as an activity, and as an opportunity to travel and socialize with old friends. However, for newcomers and for those who wish to take their birding seriously, structure and support are available, thanks to those who have struggled before them to put it in place, and those who work today to maintain it.

CHAPTER 8

Philosophical Differences

"Those goddamned birders. They can all go to hell!" Gerry heard him mutter as he signalled for her to pass. She was upset as she turned out of the parking area onto the road. She knew that May was hectic at Point Pelee, but why would that make him so angry? It was an overcast morning in May 2002 and she along with many others had decided to try their luck at finding the Painted Bunting at Sleepy Hollow Picnic Area. She had arrived promptly at 5 a.m. in order to be through the Park gate as soon as it opened. Calculating that the small parking lot at Sleepy Hollow would fill quickly, she was at her destination just ahead of a throng of other birders. A park warden and a summer student appeared to direct traffic and send the overflow of cars on to the next parking lot. The trail from Sleepy Hollow out to the beach quickly filled with expectant watchers. Luck was with her; she saw the bird after just a few hours, and she was elated as she manoeuvered her car out of its tight corner. "Mission accomplished," she thought, "now, on to the Tip." Her happiness was considerably dampened by the rude remark she had overheard. She knew that the atmosphere at Point Pelee had changed somewhat since her first visit in 1957, but she had no idea how resentful some of the staff had become. She wondered how things had come to such a pass.[206]

Conservationists, naturalists, and local residents have carried on a love-hate relationship with Point Pelee bureaucracy since before Percy Taverner complained about problems with his collecting permit. The story begins in 1800 and continues with twists, turns, and variations, making it a fascinating study of evolving philosophical differences over recreation, conservation, and resource management.

In 1800, Point Pelee was designated a naval reserve in order to preserve the timber that grew there for the masting of ships. By 1834, European farmers had already squatted on sections of the Point and unauthorized cutting of trees was taking place. In an attempt to control this, the government appointed Peter Conover as caretaker in 1881. However, in 1893, Everett Wigle obtained permission from the federal government to cut all Red Cedars having a butt of five inches or more out of the Point. In spite of local outcry and objections from the Merchant Marine, whose ships' captains depended on seeing the trees in order to warn them of their proximity to the Point, 11,400 fence posts and numerous logs from old or decaying Black Walnut trees were harvested before the concession was rescinded. In spite of the fact that the area had been designated as a naval reserve, for which there was a caretaker in place, few restrictions were actually observed and little thought was given to conservation.

Uninformed politicians believed that resources were limitless in the great wilderness frontier of Canada. Only with the obvious decline of the Passenger Pigeon (large flocks were no longer being seen) and the Bison did citizens begin to demand action be taken. The growing concern was such that, by 1873, spring shooting of some species of waterfowl was already prohibited by the Government of Ontario. Unfortunately, not all provinces were providing similar protection, and the British North America Act had placed natural resources under provincial jurisdiction. This was a problem as only through federal legislation could migratory birds really be protected. Finally, in 1909, a Commission of Conservation was established by the Canadian government. The responsibility of the Commission was to investigate Canada's natural resources and to submit recommendations for their development and conservation.[207]

It was before this Commission in 1915 that Taverner brought his request that Point Pelee be made a national park. Also facing that commission was Gordon Hewitt, Dominion entomologist for the Department of Agriculture. He explained the usefulness of native insectivorous birds to agriculture in destroying insect pests to the Commission and voiced his concern for their welfare. Hewitt's passion for bird conservation led him to become the chief negotiator for Canada, in which capacity he did much to facilitate the signing of the International Migratory Bird Treaty by Canada and the United States in 1916.

Also due to the increased interest in wildlife conservation around this time, organizations such as The Essex County Wildlife Association of Ontario began to appear. Jack Miner was instrumental in bringing this particular group together, and they in turn requested that the provincial government declare Miner's farm near Kingsville, Ontario, a sanctuary for migratory birds and that the federal government pay him an annual grant. In 1917, Gordon Hewitt travelled to Essex in order to address The Essex County Wildlife

Association and was taken on a tour of Point Pelee, an area which the club also wanted set aside as a sanctuary.[208] They were concerned about conservation but even more about the flow of American hunters onto the Point. Point Pelee marshes were prime locations for the fall duck hunt and the members of The Essex County Wildlife Association were hunters. They were concerned that Americans would buy the area and they themselves would be barred from it.

With the establishment of Point Pelee National Park in 1918, things changed only slightly. Although the original report of the Commission of Conservation states, "its scenic value, the southern nature of its birds and plant life, its importance as a main route for migratory birds and the exceptional opportunities it affords for the protection and encouragement of wildfowl, insectivorous and other birds, will all combine to make it an ideal area for a national reservation," it was 1937 before Sanctuary Pond became just that, a 600 acre reserve, off limits to hunters, and 1989 before duck hunting ceased entirely within Point Pelee National Park.[209]

Initially, the focus of Park management was recreation, so work on Park roads as well as the access roads into the Park got underway immediately. Obviously, conservation is a relative term: development of the Park involved not only roadwork, but also the clearing of some underbrush and dead trees and the building of bathhouses, pavilions, and picnic grounds, all with sand, gravel, and wood taken from inside the boundaries of Point Pelee. By 1925 visitor attendance had soared to forty-five thousand between May and September; most visitors came to camp, picnic, or just enjoy the beaches. Birders were few and far between by this time: W.E. Saunders was the single remaining visiting member of

*Male Chuck-will's-widow on nest at White Pine Picnic Area,
PPNP, June 5, 1977.*

the Great Lakes Ornithological Club, coming with various
friends as time allowed. But with conservation on the federal
government agenda, and the International Migratory Bird
Treaty in place, the fact that Point Pelee was a national park
on a migration flyway brought it under bureaucratic
scrutiny. Civil servants such as James Harkin (commissioner
of Dominion parks), Hoyes Lloyd (supervisor of wildlife
protection in Canada), Harrison Lewis (federal migratory
bird officer for Ontario and Quebec), Gordon Hewitt
(Dominion entomologist) and later, George Stirrett (chief
parks naturalist for national parks), all visited Point Pelee
and made it their business to be familiar with this place.

As the Great Depression descended upon North
America, Point Pelee faced even greater pressures. Its natural resources were taxed to the limit. Families now found it
cheaper to live in the Park all summer than to rent in

Windsor or Detroit. Flora and fauna were trampled underfoot and driven over by the masses of campers and visitors. Possibly due to depressed land prices, the owner of 170 acres, including an abandoned apple orchard once owned by Langille, gave up his interest in the land to Point Pelee in 1938. The Federation of Ontario Naturalists, seeing an opportunity, lobbied successfully to have this land turned into a nature reserve. In 1939, they forwarded a resolution to the National Parks Bureau, in Ottawa:

> Whereas Point Pelee National Park includes a number of plants and animals rare or absent elsewhere in Canada, and whereas changes brought about by the development of the park as a tourist resort threaten to eliminate the conditions on which the continued existence of these plants and animals depend ... Therefore be it resolved that ... areas still in essentially natural conditions be set aside as nature reserves and fenced so as to limit access of these reserves to those obtaining a permit from the Ottawa office of the National Parks Bureau.[210]

The federal government was already concerned about overuse of Point Pelee resources; so much so, that May 1939 brought with it the beginning of an ecological investigation led by officers representing the National Parks Bureau and the Forest Service, Department of Mines and Resources, and the Division of Botany, Science Service Department of Agriculture: Halliday, Senn, and Lewis. The terms of reference were:

> Conservation of the natural flora and fauna of the Park, with the making of recommendations in respect thereto, including the reservation of areas and steps towards rehabilitation ... The point of view taken by the examiners, for the Park as a whole, is that it is not a question of forest management for sustained wood production but one of maintaining the natural associations in good condition, allowing the normal course of succession to take place towards relatively stable and self-perpetuating climaxes. This maintenance in turn will act naturally in a favourable manner towards preserving the related fauna of those associations and towards affording the proper habitats for all forms of life.[211]

An immediate result of this study was that some camping areas were closed in order to allow for regeneration. This was not a popular decision among local people but it became increasingly obvious that there was a need to begin some sort of control.

If Pelee was overcrowded during the summer months, the same could not be said for April and May when birders came to watch spring migration. If they were lucky enough to be able to afford accommodation at that time, they were hard-pressed to find any. As William Gunn put it, "I can remember the May days, before Mrs. Wolfe took over, when I used to plead for a room and board at the [Aviation] Inn, only to be told that the place was just being cleaned up for the forthcoming "season" and would not open before

June."[212] Birders camped in the open, on beaches, in picnic shelters, in the old Life-saving Station, and on the porch of Post House. There were no fees as the park season had not yet begun. No one seemed to take much notice of birders and they led a fairly free and inexpensive, if somewhat uncomfortable, existence.

A second study commissioned by the Department of the Interior in 1942, and conducted by Dr. C.H.D. Clarke, who worked for the National Wildlife Branch, recognized that positive changes had been made by Park administration and suggested additional management strategies. As a result of his report, a heated meeting between The Essex County Sportsman's Association and Dr. Harrison Lewis took place on August 11. In the anger of the moment such unsubstantiated arguments as questioning the legality of the fencing off of the Nature Reserve and closing of Sanctuary Pond to hunting were put forward. Also under fire by the Association was Parks Canada's policy of bringing in "experts" rather than relying on the knowledge of long-time residents. The Federation of Ontario Naturalists, also represented at the meeting, joined in the fray, objecting to any increased hunting. Citizens of Point Pelee claimed that naturalists were trying to monopolize the Park, with the goal of excluding the general public. Bert Girardin called W.E. Saunders a "game destroyer" and objected to the collection of specimens in the Park for scientific research. This was the same local hunter who was so willing to help the Great Lakes Ornithological Club members collect birds and data in the early 1900s! Freedoms to which Point Pelee residents were accustomed were being denied, and at this meeting they showed in no uncertain terms that they did not like it.

As time went on several things happened that brought

about new problems for Point Pelee. Wind erosion in the camping, picnic and parking areas destroyed vegetation and exposed sand. Storms eroded beaches, particularly East Beach. Attendance at the Park continued to increase, and the administration began to enforce the regulations in all seasons for all visitors. The increase in birder numbers began to cause concern over possible harassment of birds and damage to the environment. A decision was made to buy all privately owned land on the Point and return it to its "original" form. And, as a result of all the changes, environmental and managerial, the growing Park bureaucracy was losing touch with local and visitor needs.

The least divisive of these issues was shore erosion. As early as 1915, the federal government was alerted to the problem through Taverner's report to the Commission of Conservation in Ottawa. He claimed that serious shore erosion at Point Pelee was due to off-shore removal of sand deposits, and he supported residents in their call for a ban on all sand removal from the bottom of Lake Erie. But nothing was done and the erosion continued. Richard Saunders described the erosion he saw during a trip to Pelee in May 1946:

> It did not take us long to discover that the Point has been further eroded this winter, astonishingly so. More than half of the tree and scrub-bearing area has now been destroyed so that another season or two of this devastation will endanger the life-saving station and the adjoining buildings. The pale, barked skeletons of willows on the sands are mute witness of the steady encroachment of

the lake. Since the largest of these trees must have been at least 15-20 years old, this eroding process has reversed a building-up of the point that must have gone on for a generation or more. ... We planned to drive down the east road beside the marsh in the afternoon so I told Tom to tell Greer to pick me up somewhere along that road. But when I reached the beach where the road turns north I found to my astonishment that the road had been entirely washed away for a hundred yards at the bend! Some piles had been driven into the sand at this point, evidently to try to stop the washing but without success.[213]

A comment from Don MacDonald made two years later completes the picture: "At 1:30, Bill Smith, Bill Giles and I ... bunked under the pavilion (by the life saving station) which used to be in the centre of the tip, and now is on the east beach, filled with about one foot of sand."[214]

Meanwhile, the erosion of East Beach continued in spite of attempts to prevent it or slow it down. "Between 1949 and 1953 approximately $85,000 was expended by the National Parks Branch on various experimental beach protection methods."[215] The methods were not working and another investigation was done in 1964 by Dalton Muir, park naturalist with the Department of Northern Affairs and Natural Resources, who stated: "It is a well known fact ... that the point is about three-quarters of a mile shorter than it used to be. ... Heavy storms from the southwest and northeast seem to do heaviest damage. The National Research Council in Ottawa is currently working on a project to produce effective breakwaters to reduce the pounding of the waves."[216]

In spite of all the efforts being made, East Beach near the Visitor Centre and East Point Beach, now simply known as east side of Tip, vanished, as had the Life-saving Station before them. Bill Clark, a long-time birder to Point Pelee, described these changes:

> A road from the Visitor Centre led down to a boat ramp and a parking lot at East Beach. This road also connected to a track which followed the shoreline northwards for a few kilometres. There was also a washroom facility for beach users. The trail past the entrance to Tilden's woods continued on to the beach. I often used this trail and the road on a round trip from the Centre as the birding was always rewarding. Violent storms dumped tons of sand onto the road and parking lot. ... The facility was removed and the road closed off at the Visitor Centre. ... East Beach is no longer shown on park maps. ... the south train stop [at] East Point Beach ... was destroyed and its sand dumped over the loop road. It was bulldozed clear, but the problem with the unstable area remained. It was decided to abandon the loop road and reroute the train to the more stable west side. The washrooms and change rooms were removed and East Point Beach, the last such recreation beach on the east side of Point Pelee was closed.[217]

The erosion problem created a space problem. Point

Entrance to the Woodland Nature Trail late 1950s.

Pelee was small and getting smaller; something had to be done to accommodate the increased number of visitors. Dr. Hugh Keenleyside, Deputy Minister of Mines and Resources, kicked off another extensive study of wildlife in all national parks in 1949. John S. Tener, trained in ecology and wildlife management at the University of British Columbia, began this work in Point Pelee because of its small size and location close to Ottawa. In part, his interim report stated:

> Point Pelee was set aside as a national park primarily because of its unique fauna and flora and not because of its suitability as a picnic and bathing ground for local inhabitants. The forces of conservation and recreation are diametrically opposed because of the small area involved and the large number of visitors

to the park. The time has been reached where a decision must be made as to whether the purpose of the Park shall be for recreation or for preservation of fauna and flora. ... The following recommendations ... are respect-fully submitted ... That all private land within Point Pelee National Park be expropriated ... That waterfowl hunting season be perma-nently closed ... That no overnight camping be allowed ... That the Park close at 11.00 p.m. ... That beaches be patrolled ... That 50 Wood Duck nesting boxes be constructed ... That a nature guide be employed during the summer months.[218]

Tener was encouraging Parks Canada to redress the balance between recreation and conservation.

At the time of Tener's report there seemed to be no reason for birders or naturalists to be concerned about their freedom within Park boundaries. Unlike the escalating summer numbers, there weren't overwhelming numbers of birders making the trip to Point Pelee in the early 1950s, and birding was also seen as a benign activity compatible with conservation. However, with more money available, better transportation, more leisure time, better equipment, and better field guides, the popularity of birding began to soar. Point Pelee felt the pressure of this increase, and management was beginning to look at ways to deal with the sheer numbers. Fred Bodsworth watched the changes taking place with a mixture of trepidation and understand-ing:

We also put a tent up in one of the picnic areas and then somebody came and told us that the ranger had been around and let our tent down. Once my wife and I were going to sleep in the station wagon—those days at the Tip were just trails through the woods that you could get off the main road with a car or a station wagon. We were back in the woods preparing to sleep overnight and the ranger came along and asked if we were planning to spend the night there. I said yes we were and he very politely said that we should use the campground as there were more convenient facilities there. After being footloose and free to go where you wanted and do what you wanted, the birders who had been going there for years rebelled for a while at this regimentation. But now there were too damn many of us and it was necessary.[219]

Meanwhile, Park administrators, hoping to alleviate some of the overcrowding, began an intensive program of land acquisition with the purchase, in 1956, of eighty lots in a registered subdivision. Aviation Inn was bought and it, as well as Point Pelee Lodge, were closed and torn down. Now that Dr. Stirrett was the chief parks naturalist of Canada, interpretation and education became part of the national park mandate. Rowley Frith, a naturalist from Ottawa with a biology degree from the University of Guelph, was hired as interpreter in 1960 and was well liked by visitors. Ron Steele, reporter for the *Windsor Star* wrote about Frith in glowing terms:

If you have toured the nature trail, chances are
he met you in the nature preserve and tipped
you off about what flowers or birds to look for
and where you would most likely find them. If
you have watched movies at the campsite
theatre, he was the man showing the films and
offering a running commentary. If you had a
question about the nature of things in the park
it is probable that he gave you the answers.[220]

With education and interpretation taking place, increasing numbers of visitors came to understand the ultimate role
of a national park and Point Pelee seemed to be headed in
the right direction.

Unexpectedly, Point Pelee National Park management
was delivered a shock in 1962, when the *Glassco Royal
Commission Report on Federal Government Organization*
recommended that Point Pelee National Park be dropped
from the national park system. Their reasoning was that
Point Pelee, Georgian Bay Islands, and St. Lawrence
Islands, have "little in common with other federal parks
either in the nature of their operations or their utility in
terms of conservation or the attraction of tourists. ... A
complete review of national park policy should be undertaken and operational patterns developed which may best
harmonize the twin objectives of meeting the recreational
needs of the people and preserving the natural beauty and
character of the environment."[221] It is unclear what the
Commissioners thought was wrong with Point Pelee: visitation was high, interpretation was taking place, many forms
of recreation were available, and the operating cost per visitor was low. Fortunately, Essex County politicians, along

with local Member of Parliament Eugene Whalen, won the fight to retain Point Pelee's national park status.

In 1965, when William Wyett was hired as a full-time naturalist, plans began for an interpretive centre, the first in Canada, and Tilden's 80 acres of garden property and Point Pelee Orchards were purchased. All this activity culminated in the proposal announcement in 1967, by Harry Cooper, park superintendent, of a ten-year management plan for Pelee that was contingent on buying all remaining private land:

> The changes will include the development of a 600-unit camp area, a one-way circular road-way, cutting off about 1 ? miles of access to the actual point, restoration of natural habitat, provision of accommodation for as many as 40,000 visitors a day ... about 13% of the park will undergo development. The remaining 87% will be left in its natural state.[222]

Local naturalist Wilf Botham learned that this plan would locate much of the new campground in Anders' Field (part of the Point Pelee Orchards property) and objected. He wrote to Gerald McKeating, executive director of the FON: "This Anders' Field is a unique habitat. This year there are nesting Dickcissel and Henslow's sparrow in the field."[223] Paul J.G. Kidd (vice-president of Hiram Walker Ltd.) and Dr. James W. Wilson (a Windsor dentist), both naturalists and long-time visitors to Point Pelee, were among those who objected to the plan. Their fear was a Coney Island type of development with parking lots, campsites, service centres, and refreshment stands. Eventually that particular portion of the plan was shelved and a limit of 152 campsites was set, but the problem of high visitor use of a small area would continue, and as the Park headed into the 1970s changes were inevitable. These began in 1971 with the use of a transit system to shuttle visitors from the Visitor Centre to the Tip, closing off over two kilometres of road to other traffic from April to October inclusive. The original system, bought from Expo 67, consisted of a small tractor-style vehicle pulling open wagons or coaches. In 1982 a new system, which is still in use today, was put on the road. A Ford Bronco pulls two wagons, which are enclosed by glass on three sides. A step runs the length of the fourth side in order to allow access, and a safety bar pulls down to ensure safety of visitors.

Birders, however, were still left to find birds wherever they wished, and there were many deer trails that they found useful for getting through the bush. Tom Hince recalls that people would remind one another to be careful to avoid stepping on the flowers. But if there was a "perched bittern, you'd get a crowd of about 200 trampling around and everything would get mowed down. ... When a bird was found beside the trail, we'd get five or ten young bucks like Alan and I and go through in a line until we flushed it out and kept flushing it until even for us it would disappear." Birders were beginning to take note of a problem of their own creation and in May 1976, the FON and Conservation Council of Ontario cancelled their annual spring outings to the park. Their concern was the environmental damage done by large groups visiting the park. Peripheral problems were cropping up as well, such as difficulties finding local accommodation and parking spots close to the Visitor Centre.

By 1977, May attendance was at 59,954—the second

highest month for that year. Birders were putting pressure on Point Pelee National Park resources to the extent that a management plan was specifically aimed at minimizing negative impacts of this activity. The perceived problems addressed by the plan were disturbance of both migrant and nesting birds, damage to vegetation, and soil compaction due to trampling and "random movements of birders," resulting in many unofficial side trails: "A major factor that has contributed to these problems is that there is presently no well defined system of trails. As well, many of the trails have not been planned with the user's or a specific purpose in mind."[224]

Thus the battle of the trails began. Even amongst Park staff there was no black-and-white solution. Donald A. Wilkes, assistant chief park naturalist, stated: "I feel vegetation trampling has to be put into perspective. Definitely it is a problem in the Tip area where plant sandbinding is the key to erosion control. However, in the forest I feel the problem is overstated. Key species are not being eliminated nor is the volume trampled affecting the habitats as a unit. ... many trails used by birders are maintained by deer."[225]

Tom Hince, who was hired in November 1983 as a Point Pelee National Park naturalist, described how the decision to establish trails and keep people on them began as a method of environmental protection, but turned out to have benefits for the birders as well. Part of the trail program included free birding hikes led by a naturalist. These were designed as tools for teaching environmental ethics to young and new birders in order to introduce them to environmentally friendly birding etiquette and show them that by staying on the designated trails they could have a good birding experience. Previously, if a rare bird were found, it was likely to be flushed before many birders found out about it. Today, eighty birders can be standing on a trail, shoulder to shoulder, and the bird will walk right by them. The net result is that birds are seen better, there is less environmental impact, and more birders get a chance to see more birds.[226]

Bill Clark articulated the birders' understanding of the need for and benefits of remaining on the trails. What birdwatchers did not fail to notice however was that whole areas of the Park had become inaccessible and that trail enforcement was carried out to the point of irritation:

> We were told to stay on the marked seasonal and temporary trails. This I soon came to realize was a sensible measure. We had of course to be more patient but the birds were not chased … My greatest regret was that I was denied access to some good birding areas deep in the eastern part of the woods north of the Sparrow Field. I also did not particularly like the presence of the trail enforcement people.[227]

He was not the only one who felt this way. Wilf Botham resorted to visiting Point Pelee in the fall in order to avoid the crowds and the interference: "It was not till 19 September that I returned to Point Pelee. By then the summer madness had passed and some sanity seemed to have settled over the land. It was again possible for a simple amateur naturalist to go in and list the plants and animals without being detained by a confused youth trying to carry out orders of those in authority."[228]

Beginning in 1984, "Operation Spreadout" encouraged birders coming to Point Pelee to travel to local birding "hotspots" such as Hillman Marsh, Holiday Beach, and Wheatley Provincial Park. Although this plan was new to Point Pelee National Park, it certainly was not to bird-watchers who had traditionally birded these areas, and others, such as Rondeau. For instance, the highlight of an FON meeting in 1955 was outside Point Pelee National Park boundaries:

> One feature of the Gathering and of the weeks that followed was 'the mud puddle' as it came to be known. A large section of the marsh in the northeast corner of the Point, outside the Park, is being drained with the object of putting it into agriculture. While naturalists deplore this action, they took advantage of the way that waterfowl and shorebirds were attracted by a temporary pond and mud-flat created by the draining. It was the only spot on the Point to provide a smattering of late ducks and its vicinity was also a port of call for golden, black-bellied, and semi-palmated plovers, solitary, pectoral, semi-palmated and least sandpipers, yellow-legs, knot, and dowitchers.[229]

Regardless of the sanction of Point Pelee National Park, some local residents resented this influx of traffic onto their streets and Bill Clark remembered that "there was a report of one birder's car being pushed off a road."[230]

Meanwhile, many birders believed that a more thorough system of trails should be developed and in a letter written to the park superintendent in 1992, long-time Pelee birder

Bill Martin suggested some additions:

> More formal trails would benefit both park
> and visitors alike ... I am convinced that 99.9%
> of birders now stay on the paths be they
> formal or seasonal and that the percentage of
> Carolinian vegetation that would be affected
> by more paths would be statistically insignifi-
> cant. More formal paths are needed in the
> Post Woods, the north and east sides of
> Tilden's Woods, the old asparagus fields, the
> dunes area north of Sleepy Hollow and Dunes
> picnic areas ... In my view, garlic mustard is
> the real enemy, not birders. ... I do not think
> that "enough" trails would result in a plethora
> of trails. ... If a sort of large-scale arboretum is
> contemplated, then surely we should all be
> allowed to see what it contains.[231]

Thus the subject of trails, like a stone in the shoe, continued to irritate birders. In 1999, with the closure of a seasonal
trail connecting Tilden's Woods and DeLaurier, birders lost
access to an area in which they often found Yellow-breasted
Chat. (This trail was used by many casual visitors and was
also a cross-country ski trail in the winter months.) A sign at
the head of the trail in late May read "temporarily closed."
The consensus among birders was that there was probably a
problem with the little bridge that was part of the trail and
had been in poor repair. The following year the trail was still
"temporarily closed," but now birders were a little more
upset. This was the "chat trail" to many who were familiar
with the Park and as Bob Taylor said: "It is a source of great

annoyance to the birders as it was one of the most important trails in the park enabling birders to move from Tilden's to DeLaurier and vice-versa."[232]

By this time, the old maintenance compound had been shut, and the east road on which it was located, between DeLaurier and the Visitor Centre, was permanently closed to vehicles as well. Birders walked the old roadway and enjoyed the fact that they did not have to worry about traffic. That was a bonus—for one season only! During the off-season, that roadbed was broken out, trucked away, and replaced with mounds of messy soil and brush, dug up elsewhere and randomly dropped there. This activity allowed Park resource management to claim that a whole swath of land had been rehabilitated and the "human footprint" narrowed a little more. It did not help birders who wanted to spread out but increasingly had nowhere to spread out to! With this in mind the Anders footpath has since been developed through those "messy mounds" down the old roadbed from DeLaurier south to the cemetery, once again forming a connection between the DeLaurier and Tilden's Woods Trails.

The closing of the "chat trail" was a direct consequence of a long-term study that showed there was DDT residue in the soil in some parts of the Park. Robert M. Sachs, who worked on the Tilden farm during World War II, recalled: "We started using the marvelous new DDT to kill the flies that tormented the cows."[233] However, since the residue came mostly from the use of DDT in the orchards, old Camp Henry, DeLaurier, the maintenance compound, and the old Pelee Orchard area behind it were the only areas deemed unsafe. This led to Camp Henry being moved to the group campground, the only camping spot left in the Park. It also resulted in the closure of the maintenance compound and the move of both maintenance and the administration offices to a Sturgeon Creek property outside of the Park. Now Point Pelee administrative personnel did not even have to drive through the Park, much less keep in touch with the visitors there, and said visitors were hard to convince that all this had been necessary.

As far back as the 1970s, Wilf Botham noted a change in the relationship between Park staff and visiting birders and naturalists:

> Seeing Russ reminded me of the golden years of the 60's when the wardens Russ Dowham and Peter Tasker, the superintendent, Tony Peirce, his wife Stella, the naturalist Rowley Frith, were all on equal terms with the amateur naturalist. All or any one of them, would never be too busy to spend time with the visiting amateur. ... Now we never see the superintendent, the wardens are mostly strangers, the naturalists are so busy they have no time to establish close relations with the amateur. Of course there have been other changes ... but the most significant change so far as the amateur is concerned has been the dramatic increase in the number of amateurs visiting the Point, and the increasing competence of some of the amateurs. It would not be an overstatement to say that the amateurs are now the informed ones.[234]

The situation was not improving. Perception is everything, and the perception of an increasing number of repeat birders at Point Pelee is that they are unwelcome here. In May of 2002, a Painted Bunting was spotted hanging around Sleepy Hollow. Many birders wanted to see this bird and, in consequence, were filling up the parking spaces at that location. It was normal for Park authorities to prevent more cars from going in than there were parking spaces. That was not a problem for Tom Hince, but, as he pointed out, the job was poorly done: "it was raining heavily and the staff members ... kept the site gated, and flagged us on. We were rather miffed to find that the parking lot had no fewer than 14 empty spaces." [235]

Another decision that affected birders taken that same year was the change in closing time from 10:00 to 9:30 p.m. To a non-birder, that half hour would have meant little, but it was tradition for birders to wait in the DeLaurier parking lot for the opportunity to witness the mating ritual of the American Woodcock. The earlier closing meant that visitors could not stay to listen for Screech Owls or watch the American Woodcock display and still get out of the Park on time. To their dismay, many birders were inadvertently caught after hours in DeLaurier that year and ordered out of the Park.

Park staff, if asked, would say that they were doing a great deal for birders. Compared to what had gone on before, when birders were oddities and virtually ignored, that would be correct. They open and staff the Visitor Centre early, maintain the sightings book, provide early shuttle service to the Tip with an extra stop at the entrance to the Woodland Nature Trail, open the park gates at 5:00 a.m., and prepare washrooms in the picnic and beach areas to accommodate these early-in-the-day, early-in-the-season visitors. There are also seasonal footpaths flagged in the spring for the use of birders.

However, the Park employees' main activity was, and still is, enforcement of parking and trail use. What the birders experience are increased restrictions. In their defence, Park staff have the unwelcome job of enforcing rules over which they have little or no control. Also, birders are not innocent of infractions as this 1960s story about Fred Bodsworth and Pierre Berton illustrates:

> On one memorable Pelee trip it rained persistently, we were nowhere near the 100 tally, and we parked on what we thought was a hidden beach to drown our melancholy in a few beers. Alas, we had barely begun when an RCMP car suddenly appeared beside us. In those days, Pelee, a national park, was policed by RCMP. They gave us a choice—be charged with drinking in a public place or empty all our weekend stock of beer right there on the beach. Did you ever uncap and pour out 48 bottles of beer with two cops standing by to make sure that not a drop was left in the bottom of a single bottle? It takes a distressingly long time. ... The cops gave no indication of recognizing Pierre, but I am sure from the gloating smiles that they did. And I am sure that wherever RCMP swap stories, there are two who tell with glee of the time they forced RCMP-baiter Berton and party to pour 48 bottles of beer on the sands of Point Pelee.[236]

Stories such as this are legion and most people involved (both transgressor and staff member) are good-natured about the situation. But high numbers of birders, expanding lists of rules, and changing trails exacerbate pressure on staff in May and can lead to frustration and overreaction. Their belief that they must maintain authority also precludes friendships with the visitors.

On this point, it is fair to conclude that Park management has lost some basic contact with birders, a group of people who are generally already well-versed in environmental issues. A study of Point Pelee's birdwatchers done in 1988 found that:

> The ability to address ... issues ... depends upon the success of achieving a better and more thorough understanding of the specific user group. ... bird watchers are seen as ... a sophisticated political force ... 59.7% have bachelor degrees or greater, 14.1% hold masters degrees, 16.0% held doctorate degrees. As levels of education attainment increase the requirement for explanations ... also increases as people in higher education classes tend to be more highly independent and assess a situation before conforming or complying to the strategy or role. In addition, quality information and presentation are important if the park visitor is to take notice of and accept management strategies. [237]

This brings to mind another philosophical difference between birders and Park administration—their attitudes to the removal of exotic species. Birders have no objection to the removal of invasives such as Garlic Mustard (*Alliaria*

An aerial view of the Sparrow Field looking west in the 1960s

officinalis) or Purple Loosestrife (*Lythrum salicaria*), but
removal simply because a species is not native is not always
acceptable to them. Visitors, and former residents of Pelee
as well, "'connect" with certain plants for various reasons.
For some, a tree might be the only sign left that they had
once lived in a house here. For others, such as Bill Clark,
simple recognition of a favourite spot might be important.
"I found that my favourite lilac bushes on one of the Tilden
Woods temporary trails had been felled. A pair of fruit-
bearing peach trees growing in the area just west of the
Sparrow Field probably suffered the same fate. The lilacs
and peach trees were just as much part of the history of
Point Pelee as the much touted DeLaurier House and also
the drainage canals."[238]

Wilf Botham was "surprised and angered" to learn that
they had cut down a Siberian Elm, "which was the most
southerly woody plant on mainland Canada. It had served as

a windbreak for early spring and late fall birders watching for
rare birds that might be flying past."[239] As well as that elm,
large patches of lilacs were removed from the Tip during the
winters of 1976-77 and 1977-78. Removing these particular
lilacs opened a section of the Tip to wind erosion and gained
the Park nothing in return. Not only were they removing
human history, but they were making doing so a priority.

Other birders were particularly incensed when "exotic"
trees that were attractive to many species of migrating birds
were felled. In a 1970 report on migration, George Stirrett
cited an article by James F. Parnell, who claimed that "nearly
all parulids [wood warblers] were found to exhibit definite
habitat selection during migration. They showed a prefer-
ence for habitats similar to their nesting ones."[240] Bill
Martin, in a letter to the park superintendent, used the same
argument and offered the following suggestions:

> Point Pelee is a geophysical fact. It is also an
> internationally-recognized natural wonder. It
> is not only the Carolinian vegetation that
> draws down large numbers and varieties of
> birds during migration along the Atlantic and
> Mississippi flyways, it is the location and
> configuration of the land as well. Given this
> fact, it is surely valid to suggest that, stressed
> and threatened as many bird species are these
> days, any haven is important; that any place
> that can serve as a resting place is vital.
> Equally important for these large mixed flocks
> must surely be that they be able to find suit-
> able micro-habitats and, therefore, food, in
> the first crucial hours after they land. This

should support the case for a certain degree of mixed habitats, ... rather than the concept of a more uniform Carolinian forest. ... Ensure, then, that such things as Sparrow Field habitat be left where it presently exists. Consider retaining a few fruit trees throughout the park ... For similar reasons, I would vote for retaining the big open field at DeLaurier and Anders Field and for not planting Carolinian forest on them.[241]

Martin's statement also raises the issue of management of Point Pelee to continue to support a variety of habitats. Sparrow Field is of particular interest to birders whose disgruntled grumblings can be heard as they walk through a previously open area now almost lost to dogwood and sumac. When structures such as the administration building and those in the maintenance compound are removed, open areas are created. As with the old roadbed, the long-term plan is to plant trees in these areas rather than allow them to remain open. This is hotly contested by those such as Alan Wormington who feel that an important habitat is being lost.

I consider any opening in the Park—either new or old—to be a 'jewel' that is worth leaving 'as is' for the many rare species that depend on such openings for their survival in the Park. If such sites are left alone, through natural succession they create (for years) some excellent habitat for these rare species. ... In my opinion, the number one threat to Point Pelee right now is this mentality of consistently not recognizing that open areas—any and all open areas—form extremely valuable habitat. [242]

There are two problems involved: new open areas that are created by removal of buildings, and older open areas that are now growing back in. Many birders feel that the former should be left alone to grow in gradually, while the latter should be maintained in order to ensure that they remain open.

A government study of national parks across Canada, *Unimpaired for Future Generations*, states:

> One way to ensure that our parks are preserved ... is to educate and involve the public. By encouraging participation in various parks programs, Parks Canada can help ensure that school children, stakeholders and visitors come to appreciate ecosystem-based management and become responsible stewards of their heritage and ambassadors for national parks. ... Ecological integrity should be Parks Canada's primary ... message. [243]

Point Pelee administration commissioned a study of its own in 2000. In the *State Of The Park Report Point Pelee National Park*, ecological integrity is defined: "ecosystems have integrity when they have their native components (plants, animals and other organisms) and processes (such as growth and reproduction) intact." Next, in a statement of ecological vision, "Point Pelee National Park protects, maintains and, where possible, actively restores, a remnant example of a Carolinian ecosystem." In its list of goals and objectives

Looking down on East Point Beach showing the shuttle stop, washrooms, and food concession, early 1970s.

three areas stand out: "restore red cedar savannah community ... restore oak savannah/dune community ... eliminate aggressive [such as Garlic Mustard] exotic plant species."[244] These are all good suggestions that would be supported by most birders. However, with areas such as the old roadbed, ecological integrity for Point Pelee has, unfortunately, been equated with disturbed site restoration, and climax forest is high on the list of management goals. Regardless of the fact that *Unimpaired For Future Generations* suggests active management if necessary, including "fire restoration," and that "laissez-faire management can be inconsistent with a goal of maintaining or enhancing ecological integrity," to date no appreciable change in direction has been seen. This study panel also states that "issues regarding ecosystem-based management are complex and fraught with uncertainty. Dialogue and debate are key elements to addressing these challenges. However, we have found that the climate within Parks Canada is not conducive to either internal debate or public advocacy."[245]

It is easy for a government panel to make broad statements regarding management. But governments have not backed up these suggestions with equal amounts of funding, so lack of money is a big sticking point for many national parks. Point Pelee is no exception.

Programs to make the national parks more accessible are an example of how government funding can encourage action and be put to good use. The Point Pelee transit system has a wheelchair ramp, and in the late 1980s special funding made it possible to upgrade the washrooms and some trails to make them more accessible. Kelly Hulme and fiancé Peter spent "one weekend wandering the warbler-lined (wheelchair accessible!) trail of Pelee."[246] There are a number of wheelchair birders every May who appreciate the convenience offered by the hard-packed, wide trails and boardwalks.

With proper funding many things can be accomplished but, in the meantime, managing for climax forest is the cheapest way for Point Pelee to go. It is certainly less expensive, for example, to plant small trees than it is to conduct a controlled burn. Park staff also need to make a greater effort to explain ecological integrity. Using this term as a "buzz phrase" to cover all management decisions is not helpful. The concept is much too broad for the average visitor. There was a parallel situation in the early 1940s when the Audubon Societies began to stress ecology. Roger Tory Peterson, one of North America's greatest naturalists, said, "people do not start with an ecological concept. They acquire it through using some specific springboards such as birds, plants, or whatever in nature." [247] There is no question that the birders understand the concept, but their idea of how and where to apply it is different. For them, ecological integrity includes making sure that open places such as Sparrow Field are kept open to allow for a variety of habitats. As a government study done in 1996 shows, the majority of birders already have the environment at heart and their interest in Point Pelee is not totally selfish. Of the thirty-eight per cent of Canadians who observed or cared for wildlife, ninety per cent were bird-watchers.[248] The people who watch nature and appreciate Point Pelee are people to whom Park staff need not preach. On being hassled by the naturalist's assistant way back in 1966, Wilf Botham said, "many encounters of this kind would have a decided effect in cutting down the frequency of my trips." Although some amateur naturalists might agree with Botham, many birdwatchers will continue to come to Point Pelee. But their attitude may change from one of at least surface co-operation to one of open hostility. The loss of that special atmosphere of anticipation, celebration, and excitement at Pelee in May would be a tragedy.

CHAPTER 9
The New Collectors

Photography

"Let's get this show on the road" he says, a hint of a grin on his weathered face. He sits impatiently in the Point Pelee shuttle, camera in hand. None of your huge lenses and tripods for him. "How do you manage to take such good pictures without a tripod?" someone asks. "Don't you get tired of holding the camera? Can you really keep it steady enough?"

No problem: he was a Sarnia police officer and trained in marksmanship. A steady hand and a good eye are needed for both kinds of shooting, and James N. Flynn has them in spades. He has been coming to Point Pelee since 1969, and has been a Point Pelee National Park volunteer photographer since 1984. In that capacity, he keeps a running photographic history of Park activities, and is often called upon to attend Park functions. He is also a professional nature photographer, a business that has become more and more competitive in recent years. Where once there may have been only a dozen people taking pictures, now there are hundreds. Some of these people have "point-and-shoot" equipment and soon learn that this kind of photography is not for them. Others hope to break into the business with their newly acquired, expensive cameras and tripods. These people are often overeager, raising the ire of birders and experienced photographers alike. Many, who like Flynn have been taking bird pictures for years, are also birders and have a better understanding of proper etiquette for working with nature. For them, keeping up with technology is the challenge. With computers revolutionizing the industry, photography has become a maze of techno-speak. But for all of that, the hardest part of nature photography is still getting a clean picture of the subject. Warblers don't sit still to have their picture taken and patience might become a four-letter word. Trail restrictions at Point Pelee have also made the job harder, so when Flynn says "It's a jungle out there," he's not talking about Point Pelee's Post Woods!

As always, migrating birds and Carolinian flora and fauna are at a premium. But now collecting and shooting is being done with a camera and film, and by 1953 birders were already complaining about photographers. In the *FON Bulletin* that year, William Gunn lamented a Harris's Sparrow being "relentlessly pursued and photographed by a number of people."[249] At that time, naturalists often tried to observe—capture on film or photograph—birds during all their activities, sometimes putting at risk the very lives they were trying to understand. In the *Star Weekly*, in 1954, Hugh M. Halliday describes his attempts at taking pictures of a Yellow-breasted Chat nest at Point Pelee:

> The young were fully fledged and almost ready to leave the nest. My presence had kept the old birds away and the young had become hungry. As the parents flitted through the entanglement of shrubbery and grapevines

Jim Flynn volunteers his photographic skills for Point Pelee National Park.

where the nest was located the young fairly screeched with anticipation. Had I not been near, they doubtless would have been fed regularly and would have been quiet instead of drawing attention to themselves. It never occurred to me that the enemies had also been watching. As I peered through a narrow slit in the hide waiting for the old birds to come within the focus of my camera, the nest began to shake and to tilt over. Soon I noticed a fox snake looping its scaly dimensions over the side of the nest.

Repairing the nest and feeding the little birds to keep them quiet, I went back to the hide, conscious of the presence of snakes. Now the old bird, true to her tradition, began to view the situation with more suspicion than ever. When she did come with food, she was in such a hurry you scarcely got a glimpse of her. Several times she dropped the food and flew away. In the meantime the nestlings were becoming hungrier and more active than ever. Again the nest began to tilt and sag. By the time I reached it a fox snake as thick as my wrist was looping itself round a screeching nestling. I clouted the constrictor hard, but in rescuing the nestling, the snake escaped. I was in a mood to pound it to jelly. ... I rebuilt the nest in a higher and more secluded spot. After the youngsters were fed they contentedly settled down while I gathered up my equipment and cleared out in the interest of their survival. From an undisturbing distance I watched through field glasses the parents regularly going to the nest with food. All appeared normal.[250]

This kind of thing could not happen at Point Pelee today. Off-trail wandering is not allowed, permission to work freely in the Park, and research permits are hard to come by. However, in the intervening years, as photographers became more numerous, they increasingly angered birders who felt that photographers disturbed the birds by getting too close, using flash, and chasing them.

In a couple of his columns in the *Globe and Mail* from the 1980s, Peter Whalen discussed the change in numbers of photographers: "That mountain has finally been measured. Professor James Butler of the University of Alberta is surveying birder economics. The growing army of bird photographers exposes 1.7 million frames of film at Point Pelee in May, he said. Each averages 55 pictures a day. The cost of buying and developing all the film is $710,000."[251] Whalen is quick to point out that there are two kinds of photographer, those who care about the well-being of their subjects and those who don't:

> Skilled photographers who know birds accounted for much use of film. They ruffled the feathers of neither birds nor birders. But somehow, other people who would not push forward with binoculars take new cameras as a license to march in on a displaying bird. Other birders, so far, are masochistically polite. Ten or 20 may stand back, to avoid frightening the bird. They watch one man shove much closer with a camera, at risk of chasing off the bird they are trying to watch. They say nothing. A decade ago three cameras might be focused on a bird. Today, 300 can be aimed at a rarity. So far, a new etiquette has not arisen to meet the changed circumstances.[252]

By 1987, twenty-nine per cent of the visitors to Point Pelee in May were photographers.[253] Birdwatchers are quick to criticize them for their perceived bad behaviour, or their too aggressive pursuit of birds, or the flashes going off and disturbing birds and watchers alike. It could be argued that these pictures are necessary as the skins and collections of earlier days were; that only with photographs can bird books and nature magazines continue to improve; that only with the aid of excellent photographs and video footage can environmentalists convince an increasingly urban population that here we have something worth protecting.

Peter Alan Coe, from Dorset, United Kingdom, is a "twitcher" (a birder willing to travel at the drop of a hat to see a rare bird) turned photographer. In the UK in the early 1970s he was in the top thirty birders and in 2003, after twenty years of not chasing birds outside of his own county, is still in the top five hundred of approximately a million members of the Royal Society for the Protection of Birds. He travelled to Point Pelee in 1998, 1999, and again in 2003 to photograph warblers. His history gives him a perspective on both sides of the discussion. When asked "Why Point Pelee?" his response was that Point Pelee is internationally recognized as the absolutely, without fail place to go in the spring, mainly because of the warblers:

> You can never tire of North American warblers in spring plumage. In Europe we get North American warblers as vagrant birds in September or October in drab plumage ... to see that bird in spring plumage ... hopping around at your feet, Point Pelee is the place to come. I saw a Canada Warbler today for the first time in five years and spent two or three hours trying to get a decent picture ... Particularly as photographers we are trying to get good photographs of warblers, tanagers, vireos and birds like that. ... You're trying to photograph and you get this crazy situation down there—if East Tip Beach is quiet, all the birds are there—all the birdwatchers stand on

the shoreline, so to get past them, you either get your feet wet or walk across in front of them and then they get upset ... At least seventy per cent of the photos taken—even by the professionals—go straight into the bin ... If something rare turns up like that Nelson's Sharp-tailed Sparrow, you've got a tremendous volume of birdwatchers who are all trying to look at the same bird. I did not go near it for at least two hours and when I did, I found six photographers on the beach trying to manoeuver over all those boulders. The bird came out after a half hour, sat on a stone for about one second ... another twenty or thirty minutes and it came out again and sat on the stone for about thirty seconds and I got some shots. Robert McCaw, who was also there, had his tripod on one boulder with one leg, another boulder with the other leg and if he'd let go of the camera, the whole thing would have tipped right over. Most of the fellows don't use flash outside of Point Pelee. They come here specifically to get birds and if the light is no good they have got to have some extra form of lighting ... For example, the Yellow-bellied Flycatcher nests in swamp marshlands on the ground and is never seen on the breeding grounds because it is habitat that people don't go into. This makes Point Pelee a good place because you see birds out of habitat and at ground level.[254]

Photographers on East Point Beach near the Tip, May 2003.

Joanie and Norman Piluke from Toronto agree that bird photography is difficult under the circumstances found at Point Pelee. Nonetheless, they come during the rush of birding because they spend time socializing and meeting old friends as well as working. Although Joanie is a photographer, and for a while a videographer as well, her first love is locating the birds. She knows from experience that a photographer can go home with nothing. She reminds birders that photographers also have a passion for birding and that most of them know all their birds: "They work really hard—that is their job, passion, or hobby and some of them depend on it. ... Photographers feel they haven't seen the bird if they haven't captured it on film."[255]

Ron Austing from Texas avoids the May rush. Beginning in the early 1960s, Austing came to Point Pelee to photograph and video hawks in late September and early October. In his opinion, when the conditions are right at Point Pelee, "it is amazing what you can see, if you are willing to spend the time." On one memorable occasion he managed to get a video clip of a Peregrine Falcon eating a Blue Jay: "We witnessed this falcon just eating the entire jay right down to the feet, which it swallowed."[256] These days, when Austing comes to Point Pelee in the spring, it is during the first week of May. There are already a number of good birds here then, but it is not as busy as the second week.

Digital cameras have added a new dimension to photography. The pictures can be seen a second after they are taken, so a bad picture can be discarded without the cost of developing. Pictures can also be copied and printed with the use of a home computer. This combination of camera and computer has led to an increase in the number of amateurs trying their hand at nature photography. Norman Piluke has kept up with the new technology: he uses a digital camera with built-in stabilizer so he does not need to lug around a tripod, which gives him the advantage of freedom of movement—an advantage indeed!

Obviously, photographers are legitimate users of Point Pelee. They cannot be ignored or banned, but their increasing numbers have created a need for new guidelines. Whatever the future holds for bird photography in Point Pelee, one hopes that all those who enjoy birds and nature can keep the lines of communication open in a spirit of tolerance and co-operation. Tiny Point Pelee has no room to spare for strife.

Tourism

The shuttle driver gets ready to pull out of the Visitor Centre circle and a group leader hurriedly calls together his scattered flock. In the shuttle English and French are heard, with accents giving away places of origin: Quebec, the Maritimes, Ontario, United States, Britain, and Australia. Some Dutch, German, and Japanese filter through like the buzz of the hummingbird in a morning chorus of sparrows. Behind the Visitor Centre the coffee, bagels, and doughnuts are being sold quickly. A lineup of birders wait their turn, while others stand around with coffee mug in hand, or find a spot at the nearest picnic table. It is 8:00 a.m. and some of these people have already been here for two hours. They have taken the shuttle to the Tip and back and are now warming up or getting breakfast. Some have just come in from their motel and are ready for a "wake-up" cup of coffee before heading out to the Tip. As the newcomers arrive, they call out to old friends whom they have not seen since last year. They mingle, chat, move on and mingle again in a spring ritual that rivals that of the migrating birds.

Point Pelee is the destination of choice for individual birders, naturalist groups, birding organizations, national and international birding tours, family groups, and even ornithological study groups from universities and colleges. It began with W.E. Saunders, who brought first the American Ornithologists' Union from Detroit, where its annual convention was taking place, in October 1931; then the Federation of Ontario Naturalists for their annual convention in the fall, beginning later in the 1930s. In October 1949, Keith Reynolds, writer for the *London Free Press* wrote:

> All day Sunday Point Pelee, the southernmost part of mainland Canada, was firmly in the hands of four or five hundred invaders who came by bus and car from every corner of the United States. The sudden influx was a field

Hawkwatching at the Visitor Centre parking lot is serious business.

trip sponsored by the National Audubon Society on the occasion of its 45th annual meeting, held for four days in Detroit—the first time this meeting has been held outside New York City. Of all the places in North America renowned for their abundance of bird-life during spring and fall migration, none is better known than Point Pelee so, it was fitting that this ornithologists' convention should take advantage of its meeting so close to Pelee and make it the focus of its one day of outdoor activities.[257]

Thus, North American ornithological organizations continued to bring their annual meetings and their members to Point Pelee. When the Federation of Ontario Naturalists held its 1953 regional meeting at Point Pelee in

May, nine federated clubs were represented and 140 people attended. That same weekend there were over one hundred members from the Detroit Audubon Society visiting the Point as well. William Gunn, writing in the June 1953 *FON Bulletin* observed, "Indeed, for those who like to stay at the Aviation Inn, it is now a matter of booking about a year ahead to be sure of having reservations when you want them." Already, birding tours had become a thriving business.

As Wilf Botham indicated in his notes, August 27, 1960, Europeans were also making the trip to Pelee: "The American Ornithologists' Union had been holding meetings all week at Ann Arbor [and went on a field trip to Point Pelee] ... all the big names were there, some from other countries, Europe especially."[258] In 1963 the FON brought their people to the Point, and Rowley Frith, first naturalist hired at Point Pelee, writing in the *Ontario Naturalist*, was pleased to note:

> On May 12, the Sunday of the Federation gathering ... over one thousand binocular-equipped naturalists were on the Woodland Nature Trail in the Nature Preserve. Before daybreak the parking lot was filled with cars and when in mid-afternoon they began to thin out again, some of the tired but exhilarated observers were comparing check-lists of more than one hundred species. Some of the keen-eyed experts had identified twenty-five species of warblers which included such rarities as Golden-winged Warbler, Blue-winged Warbler, Brewster's Warbler, Connecticut

Warbler, Hooded Warbler and Yellow-breasted Chat. ... When Point Pelee National Park attracts thousands of naturalists as it does annually in the month of May and again to a lesser degree in September, it is undoubtedly serving the purposes for which it was originally intended.[259]

Tom Hayman adds, "This coming weekend [May 1975] the American Birding Association holds its biennial conference at Point Pelee—first time in Canada. The convention begins Thursday afternoon with a general meeting of the members at 4 p.m. at the Interpretive Centre."[260] Although many of these birders were attending conventions or club meetings, other birders were coming to Point Pelee on their own. As Peter Whalen pointed out, "On one day, license plates from eight Canadian provinces and 16 U.S. states filled the parking lot ... to illustrate the attraction for birders. Hotel and motel rooms are booked for miles around; happy Leamington merchants who rarely watch birds but appreciate the business reacted this spring with banners across the town's main intersection welcoming birders (and their wallets)."[261]

Now, birds were not the only thing being studied. Birders, what they bought, where they went, and how much they spent were also under the microscope. In Jack McKenzie's 1968 article in the *Globe and Mail*, "Here's Why Birders Watch," he quotes James Woodford, executive director of the Federation of Ontario Naturalists:

Binocular sales are up tremendously ... The Federation's equipment sales to members

jumped 50% last year. Its *Ontario Naturalists'*
Guide came out in 1964, sold a 5,000 first printing and is now into its third printing. ... Some
days in May 3,000 or more birdwatchers ...
flock to Point Pelee on Lake Erie. Fifteen years
ago only 200 would go to watch the thousands
of birds heading north on the Mississippi
flyway, ... about 11.5 million birders were
counted last year in the United States.[262]

Nineteen years later, the number of birdwatchers found
on a busy May day within the Park's 6.2 square kilometres
was up to 6,000. That number comes from a 1987 study of
Point Pelee National Park birders which showed that forty-
eight per cent were from Canada, forty-seven per cent from
Michigan, Ohio, and Illinois, and five per cent from
Belgium, Holland, and the UK. Some 60,000 to 80,000 gate
visits of birdwatchers were recorded during that May,
involving more than 20,000 individual visitors.[263] It was esti-
mated that eighty per cent of visitors had been here before.
Their reasons for returning were twofold: they came for the
birds and they wanted to visit with friends whom they had
not seen since the previous year. By 1987, seventy-eight per
cent of the birders coming to Pelee had been birding five or
more years, and the average previous experience of the
watchers was fourteen years. Sigrid and John McFarlan,
who have now been coming to Point Pelee for about
twenty-eight years, were once among the three per cent of
novice Pelee birders:

The very first day that we visited the park we
were birding and there was a tree that had

twenty-six different species of birds and John and I didn't know what they all were. We knew very little about the birds and we could identify very few. We were standing looking at these birds beside a man who knew what they all were and he would say "there's a Black-throated Green and that's a Parula." When we finally decided to leave this wonderful spot ... I said to John let's just follow this man if he doesn't mind because he knows what he's looking at. We asked him if he'd mind if we went along behind him and he said "of course he didn't mind." He was Al Patterson from Lambeth ... he wanted to see the Rails ... [at Hillman Marsh] ... we saw Sora and Virginia that night ... While we were there a Prothonotary Warbler appeared right by what was then the purple house. It was a wonderful day. ... we've been friends ever since.[264]

Meanwhile, the ecotourist industry continued to bring in birders from other countries. In 1987, England ranked first in percentage of citizens who were birders; North America ranked second, followed by Australia, Scandinavia, Holland, Belgium, and West Germany.[265] Peter Coe describes how tour companies work to build up a clientele: "They start off somewhere in Europe to get them hooked. The company puts together a good package—shows birders the birds that they want to see. When the birders return from that trip, they wonder where they can go next year, or next fall, if they are wealthy. The trips get progressively more expensive, to locations that are further away and harder to get to."[266]

Photographers in the woods.

North American birders can and do get into the same round of birding tours as those described by Coe. Agencies compete to show birders exotic species in such places as Africa, South America, and Southeast Asia, on tours led by prominent ornithologists.

In 1999, the American Birding Association (ABA) conducted a survey of its membership that explored the popularity of birding trips. Of their members, eighty per cent take at least one birding vacation a year, fifty-seven per cent expected to take an organized birding tour in the ABA area within the next few years, and thirty-five per cent expected to take an organized birding tour outside the ABA area within the next few years. Along with the tours, eighty-six per cent said they are likely to purchase clothing, eighty-five per cent are likely to purchase airfare, thirty-three per cent are likely to purchase binoculars and scopes and fifty-three percent are likely to purchase computers and software.[267]

Large tour companies and birding organizations are not the only ones taking groups out to Point Pelee and elsewhere to birdwatch. According to Patrice Turcotte, students from Laval University, Quebec City, came to the Park in May for twenty-five consecutive years, from 1974 to 1999. Since keeping lists is part and parcel of the birding experience, Turcotte reported the group's results for the last eighteen years: The lowest number of species seen, 80, was recorded in 1994, and the highest, 132, in 1991.[268]

There are families who make Point Pelee in May an annual event. Babies in backpacks, children, and adolescents, sometimes reluctant, are accompanied by parents trying to instill their own philosophy about, interest in, knowledge of, and enthusiasm for birding in their children. It is a tall order, but parents who persist will often happily find themselves left behind by intelligent youngsters who go on to make birding a career. One family who made Pelee a yearly tradition is Carol McNall's:

> I started taking my children, Kristina, Rob, and Tom out of school for an educational day at Point Pelee. I would pack the van the night before with blankets and pillows, food and treats and a yearly adventure was born. I would get them up at 3 a.m., put them back to sleep in the van and head out to be here at dawn. They loved it. One carried the bird book, one the flower book and one the tree book. We wandered the trails together. We had snacks and a picnic lunch and napped together and headed home at dark tired and

happy. ... I went in May 1977, heavily pregnant with Kati and then in May 1979 nursing three-month-old Mathew. So the adventure grew to five kids and myself. One spring I was interviewed by CBC radio with all five kids, one in a stroller, all with binoculars.[269]

Whoever they are, the desire to spend May at Point Pelee is the common denominator for collectors, whether they collect people for a trip, photos for a portfolio, or new birds for a life list.

CHAPTER 10
From Various Desks

Dr. George Stirrett shuffles through the papers on his desk, looking for a particular quote from Percy Taverner, one of the members of the Great Lakes Ornithological Club. He had been at this for years—following up old leads, ruining his eyesight trying to read handwritten letters and notes, piecing together as many of the GLOC bulletins as he could find, gradually accumulating information. He locates the paper that he is looking for and reads it over once again. He is trying to discover if Ernest Thompson Seton, the famous nature writer, ever actually birded at Point Pelee. There is sketchy information from Taverner indicating that Seton was planning a trip, but no description of the visit. He realizes that he will have to search further in order to answer that particular question. He rifles through some papers and chuckles as he reads W.E.'s description of problems encountered while collecting three Henslow's Sparrows: "I would not like to injure the reputation of the members of the camp as wing shots but certainly we used more than three cartridges."[270] Stirrett was a writer with a particular passion for Point Pelee. He compiled information on the Great Lakes Ornithological Club, kept lists of birds seen here—the "Stirrett Files," which are now held at the Point Pelee National Park Visitor Centre—and was involved to some extent in the bird-banding station, especially its move to Long Point. He wrote a column for the *Chatham Daily Star* and occasionally for the *Windsor Star* under the pseudonym "Graham Vail." Stirrett compiled a set of four pamphlets called *The Spring (Winter, Summer, Autumn) Birds of Point Pelee National Park*, which were published in 1960 by the Department of Northern Affairs and National Resources, National Parks Branch, and sold for twenty-five cents each. The spring book begins with a table of contents, then an introduction in which Stirrett explains how to use the booklet. Next, he writes about "Special Ornithological Events," including the arrival of migrants and reverse migration then in; "Observation Sites," he describes the Tip, Woodland Nature Trail, Pelee Marsh, and the farms and Onion Fields. Finally he launches into the list of birds with sighting dates and status: common, uncommon, very common, abundant, resident, or transient. At the end of this book, Stirrett includes an excellent fold-out map that gives a key to Park vegetation and shows areas in which interesting flora and fauna are most likely to be located. A couple of pages are dedicated to these plants and animals and the last two pages discuss the history of Point Pelee. These books, which were reissued in 1973 by Information Canada, were a handy reference guide for anyone visiting Point Pelee at any season of the year.

In 1966, Stirrett compiled an annotated bibliography of all articles that discussed Point Pelee National Park and the Point Pelee region for the National Parks Branch of the Department of Indian Affairs and Northern Development. It is thorough and useful for anyone working on the history of this particular area. Stirrett also wrote a report in 1970, *Point Pelee National Park: A Migratory Pathway for Birds and Insects*. The report makes it obvious that Stirrett spent a great deal of time studying all aspects of Point Pelee: who came and when, birds in migration, reverse migration, bird banding, insects, insect studies done, collections and collecting. Dr. George Stirrett was a civil servant but he held Point Pelee close to his heart. He enjoyed his journey of research into the Great Lakes Ornithological Club and very much wanted to make its history come alive. But thinking it over, he decided that writing the history was not a job that he could do and that someone else would have to take over.[271]

Thus Dr. George Stirrett fades out and John L. Cranmer-Byng steps in. Cranmer-Byng was a history professor at the University of Toronto who had just retired. He was also a birder, and he shared Stirrett's interest in the GLOC. With the aid of Stirrett's research, Cranmer-Byng wrote "The Great Lakes Ornithological Club: The Origin and Early Years, 1905-1911," which was published in *Ontario Birds* in 1984. A follow-up article, "The Bulletin of the Great Lakes Ornithological Club, 1905-1909," appeared in *Ontario Birds* in 1985. Cranmer-Byng co-edited Ornithology in Ontario in 1994 with Martin K. McNicholl, and finally wrote *A Life With Birds: Percy A. Taverner, Canadian Ornithologist*, in 1996. Stirrett could rest easy; the history that he wanted to be written was in good hands and his research had been well used.

W.E. Saunders was a prolific writer, preparing articles for various bulletins over a span of more than fifty years. Much of this writing was quasi-scientific in nature, discussing information and statistics acquired at Point Pelee. He also wrote a column called "Nature Week by Week" in the

London Advertiser, later the *London Free Press*, which began in 1929 and ran until his death in 1943. Of the 646 articles written for the London paper during those years, 118 mention Point Pelee.[272] Saunders was able to use words to paint a picture, all the while providing information and statistics useful to any naturalist. In a column about the migration of Evening Grosbeaks, Saunders observes, "In the winter of 1910, when these birds occurred all over Ontario, I found them in large numbers at Point Pelee, and my recollection is still vivid of the lovely picture made by the male birds feeding in the red cedars under the dazzling sun of a Point Pelee winter day."[273]

Keith Reynolds replaced W.E. Saunders in the *London Free Press*, with his column "Mostly Birds." Like W.E., he often wrote about May visits to Point Pelee in his column. After attending a series of lectures in London, the last of which was a presentation by the renowned Roger Tory Peterson, Reynolds wrote:

> In this part of Ontario we all make as many trips ... as we can, and most of us look upon it [Point Pelee] as one of the best places to see birds in migration in the province. But that it should have made such an impression on Peterson, who knows birds and birding all over the continent, came as a real eye-opener to me. Apparently Point Pelee is even better than I thought![274]

In May 1950, he wrote,

> I can't recall that I was ever able to record 121

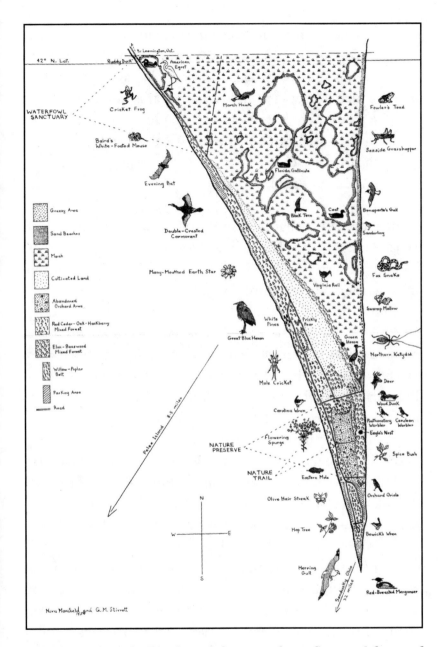

This 1958 map by Dr. George Stirrett, shows flora and fauna of Point Pelee.

species of birds in a single day before. Yet we made no special attempt to list as many birds as possible. If we had, the list could have been much larger. An indication of this was the astounding total of 141 made by three ornithologists on Saturday. Little wonder I heard two chaps making tentative plans for Pelee Weekend, 1951.[275]

In more ways than one, Reynolds was a "follower" of W.E. Saunders, but he went on to make his own career as Deputy Minister of Lands and Forests and finally retired from writing "Mostly Birds" in 1963.

Tom Hayman, knowing that the *London Free Press* would be looking for a new natural history writer, asked to be considered as a replacement for Reynolds. Hayman was given the job and he, like his predecessors, often used Point Pelee as a topic for his column. Even winter could produce newsworthy birds, as Hayman pointed out on January 9, 1975: "It might have been just another woodpecker tapping in the distance in a tangle of wild grape vines. But in fact the bird that Dave Currie spotted on the Point Pelee Christmas Bird Count Dec. 24 was a Northern three-toed woodpecker—the first such bird ever recorded in Point Pelee National Park."[276] In 2003, Hayman celebrated 40 years of writing for the London paper. The longevity of this column attests to both the ability of the writers and the interest of the readers. In the late 1990s, when the *London Free Press* changed ownership, Hayman was given two-weeks notice. His readers inundated the newspaper office with emails and phone calls concerning "Nature World." He was reinstated without missing a week!

James Baillie, published over two thousand weekly "In Birdland" columns in the *Toronto Evening Telegram* between June 1931 and May 1970 without once missing a deadline. His final column was written and filed from his hospital bed just days before his death in May 1970.[277] Baillie often reported May highlights at Point Pelee. Of necessity, descriptions were at a minimum, although the scene was always nicely set as in this 1965 article:

> Hundreds of observers from all parts of Southern Ontario and from Ohio, New York and Michigan, armed with binoculars, telescopes and cameras, have been watching the bird migration this week, here at the southernmost point on the mainland of Canada. ... The May 6 feature was a spring-plumaged male Harris's Sparrow found behind Pete Sikkema's refreshment booth at the southernmost parking-lot in Point Pelee National Park. ... On May 7, with migration accelerating, a Lark Sparrow (discovered by Gordon Bellerby, Toronto, along the dyke roads north of the park), a Cerulean Warbler on the Woodland Nature trail (Howard Cramer, St. Catharines), and a Red-throated Loon off west beach north of the park gates (Vlad Trojek, Toronto) were found.[278]

Years later, Gordon Bellerby described the scene around the Harris's Sparrow sighting Baillie mentions:

> Pete's concession was a shelter on east beach

For many years Pierre Berton and Fred Bodsworth visited Point Pelee in May.

that had cooking facilities, a counter and picnic tables. It was on a weekend and thirty or forty people were there having the breakfast of bacon, eggs and coffee for which Pete was well known. Benches overturned, eggs went flying and everyone rushed around to see the Harris's. This was just when scopes were coming in and I remember seeing a half dozen of them standing there on their tripods. I went back to finish breakfast and wished I'd had a camera—it would have been a great sight![279]

When they returned, Pete Sikkema, apparently a good guy, offered them all fresh, hot coffee.

Peter Whalen, writing for the *Globe and Mail*, shows

another side of birders—their ability to poke fun at themselves—in the following paragraph:

> One hot, sunny Wednesday, two birders gave their quarry the final word. From a bare snag, that other late-May migrant, the Olive-sided Flycatcher, shouted the song that bird guides interpret as "quick-three-beers." "A fine idea," one birder said, and the pair downed binoculars for a quick trip to a pub in nearby Leamington.[280]

Whalen wrote a weekly bird column, many of which have previously been quoted, for the *Globe and Mail* from 1977 to 1999. There was a two-year interruption after he wrote an article for another Toronto paper—a fact apparently not appreciated by the owners of the *Globe and Mail*, who dismissed him. Alan Wormington then wrote for the *Globe and Mail* for approximately two years. When he could no longer do it, Whalen was reinstated and continued with the column until his death in 1999. Tom Hince was to have taken over, even coming to an agreement with John King, managing editor, but unfortunately ownership of the *Globe and Mail* changed, and a freeze was put on all modifications to editorial policy or new columns. Thus, Tom Hince never wrote for the *Globe and Mail*. He did however write for the *Windsor Star* for five years. His column focused on making birds and birding more accessible to people. He would discuss Broadwinged Hawks when they were migrating, explaining the difference between their migration strategy and that of other hawks: these birds fly six weeks without eating and go all the way to South America. Hince enjoyed writing these columns but a change of policy at the *Windsor Star* removed his column along with those of several other freelance writers.

Hugh M. Halliday, who wrote a wildlife column for more than forty years for the *Toronto Star*, as well as James MacKenzie and Fred Bodsworth, were a few other nature writers from the Toronto area who had columns and articles published in various magazines and newspapers in the 1950s and 1960s. Looking at the number of nature columns written then as compared to the more recent experiences of Hayman at the *London Free Press*, and Hince at the *Windsor Star* and the *Globe and Mail*, it is obvious newspaper publishers are under the impression that interest in natural history is waning.

The *Windsor Star* and the *Leamington Post*, under various reporters, have continually featured news of Point Pelee National Park. Such fare as the Christmas Bird Count and spring and fall migration are regular features, but often local concerns are included as well, as in this article from the *Leamington Post*, 1965:

> While the birds are flying north, members of the Federation of Ontario Naturalists will soon move south to meet them ... at Point Pelee National Park. The annual field gathering of the FON members is scheduled for May 8 and 9. ... During the weekend, the federation will operate an information booth at the entrance to the nature trail at Point Pelee. The latest bird arrivals and where they have been seen will be available. On that Saturday, a hike will be led by James A. Baillie of the Royal Ontario Museum. The affair

usually draws enough people to fill hotel and motel accommodations in Leamington. ... The park will have about one week to recover from the invasion of smelt fishermen before the onslaught of the naturalists.[281]

In a 1972 *Windsor Star* article some long-standing controversies are hinted at:

> Shotguns boomed and camera shutters clicked and binoculars by the dozen scanned treetops as duck hunters, naturalists, and bird-banders visited Point Pelee National Park during the weekend. The duck hunters, about 100 of them, were at the park for the opening day of hunting season. And the naturalists, about 100 of them members of the Federation of Ontario Naturalists, were at the park for their annual fall visit. ... while the naturalists were looking at birds, and the hunters were shooting at the ducks, another group, the Ontario Bird-banding Association, was capturing and tagging Sharp-shinned Hawks.[282]

These are the newspapers that, through their editorials and letters to the editor, also reflect local opinions of birders and of Point Pelee National Park.

If Peterson's field guides made amateur birdwatching more accessible, then guides to birding "hotspots," such as the one written in 1951 by Olin Sewall Pettingill Jr., got watchers out of their backyards and into places like Point Pelee. Although Pettingill's *A Guide to Bird Finding East of the Mississippi* largely highlights US sites, it includes Holiday Beach and Point Pelee in its coverage of the Detroit, Michigan, area. The *Audubon magazine* included a regular column by Pettingill called "Bird Finding." In the column for the March issue, "Spring Migration at Point Pelee," he states: "The variety of species you could hope to see during a day in mid-May would be dependent on the weather factors preceding it and your time and effort in searching. As many as 261 species have been reported ... About 100 of these species are rare at any time or not usually represented in May. With luck on the weather and a reasonable effort, your chances of seeing 110 to 125 species are good, more than 125 fair."[283]

The Bird Watcher's America, edited by Pettingill and published in 1965, was followed by *Roger Tory Peterson's Dozen Birding Hotspots* written by George H. Harrison. Both these books focus on North America and feature Point Pelee as one of the best places to bird. In the latter, Harrison calls it a mid-May "bird lister's paradise,"[284] while in the former, John Allen Livingston, who contributed the chapter on Point Pelee, talks about fall birding as well. Livingston was born in Hamilton in 1923, and received a degree in English, history, and languages from the University of Toronto. He became managing director of the now defunct Canadian Audubon Society and went on to write and narrate a natural science and conservation program for CBC. He first visited Point Pelee with Ron Bremner, John MacArthur, Bob Ritchie, and Don MacDonald on May 10, 1940, at 17 years of age. Don MacDonald remembered camping on the sand south of the road and meeting only one other group of birders during that stay: William Gunn and friends working on the reverse migration study. In *The Bird Watcher's America*, Livingston's description of Pelee reflects those "quieter" times:

> Each spring, in the western corner of Lake Erie, a slim finger of land becomes the concentrated onrush of countless numbers of north-bound birds. When conditions are right, wave upon wave, swell after swell, the urgent throng of migrants surges up its narrow nine-mile length to fan out through much of eastern Canada. In the fall, the finger becomes an attenuated funnel that gently pours the more leisurely drifting masses toward the Mississippi flyway. At either season, Point Pelee is Canada's most extraordinary and rewarding situation for the watcher of bird migration. ... When the night is perfectly dark and still, the marsh throbs with life. It never fails to grip me with the indefinable enchantment I knew there as a boy and happily experience yet when there is an opportunity to sit quietly alone by its edge. ... There has been insufficient observation at Point Pelee in the autumn. Admittedly, a number of people do go there at that season, but the overwhelming majority of bird watchers visit it only in the spring. This is regrettable, for the ornithologist is dependent to a very great extent on the notes of experienced amateurs. If September bird watching at Point Pelee were stepped up, many clues to migration puzzles would be

forthcoming more quickly than they are at present.[285]

Fall birding at Point Pelee was a topic for discussion for several other writers as well. In 1982, Clive E. Goodwin wrote *A Bird-Finding Guide to Ontario*, in which he described Point Pelee in May but also included a short discussion on other seasons: "On the second weekend in May nowadays it is not unusual for the loop road on the point to be closed by 8:00 AM. ... Drive down in October, however, and you could be the only birder in the park! While it is true that peak spring warbler numbers occur usually around the second week-end in May, Pelee is a fascinating place in any season."[286] In 1991, he repeats this sentiment in another book called *The Traveling Birder*, which describes Point Pelee as one of twenty best places in the world to go on a birding vacation. "Point Pelee ... is excellent in fall, although the dense vegetation at that time makes landbirds much harder to see. Another reason ... is that the Point is a major pathway in the southbound flight of accipiters."[287]

Most of the guides begin with similar descriptions of the look and location of Point Pelee, but when it comes to the birds, the details vary, sometimes reflecting subtle changes that have taken place on the Point. In a 1984 book called *A Bird-Finding Guide to Canada*, edited by J. C. Finlay, the section on Point Pelee was written by botanist and birder William J. Crins. Crins included Bobolink and Eastern Meadowlark in his short list of common breeding birds.[288] However, neither of these have nested in Point Pelee for many years due to the ongoing disappearance of "old field" habitat.

In his *A Birder's Guide to Point Pelee*, 1999, Hince takes the bird-finding guide to a different plane, dedicating the whole book to Point Pelee. In it he also talks about fall birding: "Fall birding in this part of the park [Woodland Nature Trail] is one of the region's great undiscovered treasures. There can be so many birds that it is overwhelming—even exhausting, if a good wave is moving through during your visit."[289] Other subjects he covers are the variety of habitats, the trails, the Point Pelee Birding Area, and a seasonal status of birds. Three maps are included: Point Pelee, the Point Pelee birding circle, and one showing Windsor, Essex and some of Kent County, making the book an excellent guide for new birders and first time visitors to Point Pelee.

An early version of the bird-finding guide can be found in R.M. Saunders' book, *Flashing Wings*. Published in 1947, this journal-style book includes an account of a 1946 May trip to Point Pelee. Saunders describes the places he visited, the people with whom he was travelling, and the birds that they saw. Forty-five years later, Pete and Linda Dunne put together a book in a similar vein, writing about birding trips taken during the course of one year. In their book, *The Feather Quest*, Point Pelee National Park rates a chapter: "North American birders turn out to witness the Passerine play, birding's great rite of spring. In no place do they turn out in greater numbers or with greater enthusiasm than Point Pelee, Ontario—the place where spring and birders meet. ... In spring birders go where the warblers go, and come May both head for Pelee; seventy-five thousand of the former; forty-two species of the latter."[290]

Gerry Bennett has a style of his own, writing for birders and of birders with playful irreverence. He pokes fun at himself and his peers with a tongue-in-cheek artfulness that captures birders with their hair down, describing their eccentricities. The introduction to his self-published *Wild Birdwatchers I Have Known*, written in 1977, is a good example of his approach:

> Historians and sociologists assigned to the task of documenting twentieth-century changing trends in behavior patterns of the human race will be guilty of an unforgivable omission if they fail to include some reference to the emergence and evolution of the bird-watcher as a new and significant sector of society. ... Frequently they skulk furtively through woodlots and marshlands. Even when roaming in groups, they tend to stay in relative isolation, clinging to picnic tables or huddling around Nature Trails. Occasionally flocks do appear in the open.[291]

Bennett also amused himself and his birder friends with a second volume called *More About Birdwatchers*. Bennett, who was from Woodbridge, Ontario, was also astute enough to take advantage of those same foibles making them the basis of his self-published bimonthly newsletter, *Birdfinding in Canada*. Beginning in 1981, the newsletter included places to visit, bird lists, and statistics for the top birdwatchers. At the top of "Statisticae Canadensis" 1982, is Norm Chesterfield with a world life list of 5,340 species; yet Bob Curry and Alan Wormington, each with 366 on their Ontario life lists, were ahead of Chesterfield, who only had 364 on his.[292] Gerry Bennett kept a database for the competitive listers in the birding world. For those who were interested in quieter birding, Gerry wrote a series, "Pilgrimage to Point Pelee," from September 1983 to January 1985. In this column he included all the spots he visited on the way to Point Pelee National Park, a description and map of the Park, as well as places to visit in the area. He essentially provided a relaxed birding tour of southwestern Ontario for anyone interested in following it. He described the high number of birders at Point Pelee in May like this:

> On a May weekend, there may well be a few thousand birders at Point Pelee. This has certainly never spoiled our fun. In fact, to be in the company of a few hundred (or thousand) birdwatchers is our idea of the ultimate in pleasant social surroundings. ... Making new birding friends, meeting former ones, being a part of the scene, hearing and acting upon the endless bits of news that keep passing up and down the Point on an invisible and instantaneous grapevine, are all pieces of the fascinating birding mosaic that makes each day a pleasant experience.[293]

Bennett obviously enjoyed birds, but he also understood people. His writing, a combination of information and amusing anecdote, reflects his love for birds, his delight in the company of others, and his interest in Point Pelee, the place that brought all of this together. *Birdfinding in Canada* came to an end November 1989.

Newsletters, bulletins, and journals of various clubs and organizations discuss Point Pelee, covering a wide range of topics, informing members about this place and thereby encourage them to visit. At one time the *FON Bulletin* regularly recorded Ontario bird sightings which, of course, included those from Point Pelee as well. Both birds and birders were the subject of "Worth Noting," the column in the *FON Bulletin* written by Murray Speirs in the 1950s and by Clive Goodwin in the 1960s. In a 1958 column, for example, Speirs wrote: "Norman P. Chesterfield found a Summer Tanager at Point Pelee on May 11 and again on May 18 and a Bell's Vireo there on May 13. ... Wilfred Botham listed 31 species of warblers during May near Point Pelee including Golden-winged, Blue-winged, Kentucky, Prothonotary, Connecticut and on May 31, a singing male Hooded warbler. ... Jack Livingston, Jim Baillie, Bill Smith and John Keenleyside observed a Prairie Falcon at Point Pelee in a big hawk flight on September 20."[294]

In 2001 this tradition was incorporated into *Point Pelee Natural History News* (now ceased publication), which was edited by Alan Wormington and published by The Friends of Point Pelee. "Noteworthy Bird Records" gave a "summary of noteworthy bird observations for the period ... All listed observations pertain to the Point Pelee Birding Area ... Names of cited observers are given in full for the first sighting listed."[295] A glance at the listings quickly reveals several local and, depending on the time of year, any number of visiting birders along with their particular sighting. For a timely who's who of the birding world, one has only to read through these postings for the month of May. This publication, which ran for three years and twelve issues (2001-2003), included many detailed articles on birds as well as other natural history subjects. Examples of some of the articles published include "In Search of a Chuck-will's-widow Nest" (George D. Bryant); "Brown Pelican: New to Point Pelee" (Peter S. Burke); and "The Colonial

Jim Baillie points out a bird to friends on the Woodland Nature Trail, 1960s.

Waterbirds of Middle Island, Western Lake Erie" (D.V. "Chip" Weseloh).

Rarities and fallouts are common grist for the mill. With the publication of articles such as this one, written by William Gunn for the *FON Bulletin* in 1952, it is not surprising that visits to Point Pelee in May increased and its reputation soared:

> On Friday, May 9, relatively few birds were present on the Point. Then came the grandfather of all waves. In fifteen years of visiting the Point in May, I have witnessed many waves and participated in some of the "Great Days" when birds abound. But never a day like this. ... To begin with, the wave had all the variety in the way of species that

one could ask for. The combined list of some thirty observers surpasses 150 species. ... The really spectacular thing about the wave, however, was the number of birds involved. So many birds were crowded into the terminal portion of that relatively small point of land that an adequate description is rendered most difficult. ... I have a picture of driving along the road near the end of the Point, watching an unending stream of sparrows and thrushes rising up from each side of the road and settling back again a little farther from the road margin. The general pattern of this action was strikingly like that of a bow-wave of a fast-moving ship. Then there were the warblers, which seemed to occupy every tree and bush. ... The Post Woods had to be seen to be believed. Birds swarmed in the tree canopy and understory, while scores of others rose up in successive waves practically from underfoot as one walked slowly along. ... In the neighbourhood of Point Pelee, it was clearly evident that the birds were concentrated on the Point itself, rather than along adjacent portions of the north shore of the lake, where there was little or no evidence of any wave. ... The total number of birds present on the Point was considered too astronomical to estimate.[296]

Donald Savery, of Ann Arbor, Michigan, James Baillie, William Gunn, Earl Stark, William W. Smith, and Robert

W. Trowern of Toronto, got together on the evening of this phenomenal day in order to come to some consensus about the numbers.

Fallouts of this sort are so spectacular as to be unforgettable. They are also a hike leader's dream come true. Tom Hince, speaking of the migration waves that are often a part of Point Pelee birding, says:

> When I have a group here for four days I always hope that one day is noticeably better than others so they get a sense of the rhythm of migration. That most days are quiet and all the sudden you get a surge of migrants in and it is busy, then it trickles down—and repeats. Some springs those surges are not that big, other years they are dramatic.[297]

There is a general belief amongst the "old guard" birders that there were more birds when they were visiting Point Pelee in the 1940s and 1950s. This is so strongly expressed by them that they should be taken seriously; however, it is quite conceivable that people are apt to remember the exceptional days while conveniently forgetting the many days reflected by this description of May 1954. After an influx of migrants on May 1 and 2, the

> roof fell in and bird numbers remained abnormally low from May 3 all the way through to May 23—just about three weeks of unrelieved scarcity during what is normally the peak period. ... Naturally, the disappointingly low numbers of birds put a damper on the FON

Regional Gathering held May 7-9 and, like-
wise, on the outing of the Detroit Audubon
Society on the following week-end. ... this
May can be classified as the poorest for
migrants in 20 years. ..."[298]

Tom Hince writes about the same subject in *A Birders
Guide to Point Pelee*: "Migration traps by their very nature
are not good places to monitor short term changes in bird
populations. Certainly they have some value for long term
repeated studies where trends can be detected. But the
natural range of variation hour to hour, day to day, year to
year is enormous, and the sources of variation are primarily
weather based."[299]

For Dave Milsom, one such weather-based fallout in the
late 1990s was a memorable experience:

Second weekend in May, it was extremely cold
and the inevitable fallout occurred—swifts
huddling together in a tree hole behind the
Visitor Centre, a Kentucky Warbler was walking along the wall; ... we parked mid-morning
at the Marsh Boardwalk and an Acadian
Flycatcher immediately flew under our car for
warmth ... We also found a torpid Yellow
Warbler ... A few years earlier on a similar
May day, a Scarlet Tanager walked through
my legs to eat a much-needed grub! I fed a
male Indigo Bunting bread near the old coffee
stand; an Acadian Flycatcher sat on the rail at
the train station while a Blackburnian Warbler
perched on the downspout of the building.[300]

Days like these are hard on migrating birds, but for the birders they are a dream come true. Writers can, and do, find a wealth of topics to discuss: reverse migration, bird banding, breeding bird surveys, rarities, identification, species at risk, bird numbers, birders' places of residence, abilities, needs, spending habits, behaviour, education level and income level. As evidenced by how much has been written, there is no question that Point Pelee, one small place on a very large map, has kept its position at the centre of North American birding.

CHAPTER 11
Local Involvement Coming of Age

Léa Martell stood on stage waiting for the clapping and laughter to stop and hoping that she could thank these people without getting emotional. The Ontario Field Ornithologists had just presented her with a "certificate of appreciation" and the presenter had jokingly reminded her that she had called birders "anal retentive." The laughter proved that these birders had a sense of humour—it might even have been a little sheepish as some realized that the description was, at least in their own case, apt. The Ontario Field Ornithologists were holding their Annual General Meeting in Leamington September 1999. They spent all day Saturday birding in the Point Pelee Birding Area and were now at the Dock Restaurant where the meeting was taking place. The Friends of Point Pelee and General Manager Léa Martell were being given a certificate of appreciation "for providing staff and programs that help birders visiting Point Pelee and contribute to our knowledge of birds."[301] Léa Martell started working for The Friends of Point Pelee as "Girl Friday" in 1983 and became general manager when the position opened in 1984. She had put in much thought and many long hours in order to make birding at Point Pelee a wonderful experience, so she was pleased with the recognition, especially for her volunteers, who always worked extra hard during May. Those very loyal and helpful assistants were local residents who cared about the Friends, Point Pelee, and birders, and wanted to help in any way that they could.

For many years local involvement in the study of birds consisted mainly of offering shelter and friendship to visiting naturalists. Sometimes local residents offered reports of birds that had to be deciphered by more experienced birders. For example, from descriptions given to Dr. Brodie in 1879 of "War Birds," he understood that the Northern Cardinal was extending its range north. Other times, local residents were able to confirm for birders that phenomena they had witnessed were regular occurrences on the Point. A letter written in 1943 by Dr. Sloane, a local photographer and hunter, was quoted by Keith Reynolds in the *London Free Press*. Sloane told of a hawk migration during which the "hawks appeared from … the base of Point Pelee and traveled westerly in a continuous stream for about an hour. I counted 139 in sight at one time. There appeared to be all kinds with more of the big red-tails than usual."[302] On the other hand, the members of the Great Lakes Ornithological Club seemed to be hesitant about accepting local sightings and records. Bert Girardin, who helped them acquire specimens, and spent a great deal of time with them, was nevertheless kept outside their charmed circle. Wallace Tilden, another Pelee resident, made it his responsibility to contact W.E. Saunders when there was some bird of interest at Point Pelee. Also, he was knowledgeable enough to be a speaker at a Federation of Ontario Naturalists Regional Gathering in 1937. Why, with all the information and specimens given to the naturalists in the early 1900s, were none of the local amateurs ever invited to join the GLOC?

Pete Sikkema's breakfasts at the East Point Beach restaurant were much appreciated by hungry birders.

Maybe they were not practiced enough in natural history to aspire to the level of GLOC membership, but their association with these people inspired in the residents an empathy for all naturalists. Robert Sachs recalls staying with the Tilden family, ostensibly to work on their farm, but he did not let that stop him from doing some birding on the side:

> During WWII, the government of Ontario encouraged high school students to volunteer for farm work. In 1943 I was 16 years old and a student at North Toronto Collegiate Institute. In late April, I received a letter from a birding friend, John A. Crosby (who was even then an accomplished artist and later illustrated Godfrey's Birds of Canada). In the spring of 1943, John had started working for

the Tildens, on their farm in Point Pelee National Park. He decided he wanted to find other work that might allow him more free time to pursue birding. He suggested that I write the Tildens and apply to take his place. Happily my application was accepted and it changed my life. The Tilden family on my arrival consisted of "old" Mrs. Tilden, her two adult sons Ross and Don, and Don's wife Jo.

I fell in love with the Point (and also fell in love with Eleanor Simpson, who later became my wife of 50 years and still counting) and returned to the Tilden's farm for an additional two years of farm work. Don and Jo Tilden later invited me back as a guest while I was studying engineering at the U of T.

Spring birding during the war years was certainly different ... gas rationing assured that crowds were never a problem ... Bill Gunn was busy in the vicinity for a few days while he recorded the songs of a Bewick's Wren that had nested under the Mawhinnie cottage close to the Tilden farm house. ... I recall around 1946, walking through the Tilden's woods and onto the Aviation Inn's asparagus field and being excited to find a Black-billed Magpie flying by with long tail streaming. ... Sometimes on early mornings in the late spring there would be numbers of exhausted song birds resting on the extensive asparagus fields and hedgerows, recovering from their long night flight across the lake.

After we finished the morning asparagus cutting, we loaded the full crates onto an old Model-T Ford Truck to take them back to the shed to trim, sort and pack them for shipment. One day the Barn Swallows nesting above us in the open rafters started flying about twittering around us. Looking up we saw a very large Fox Snake in the rafters. It was methodically swallowing the young nestlings from one of the nests. The resulting 4 or 5 bumps in the snake's body were clear evidence of the snake's success.

One of my chores was to find the cows in the Tilden's woods and drive them back to the barn for milking. Ross and Don never complained about my taking a rather long time to find the cows.[303]

The farmers on Point Pelee would have a continued impact on visitors as they welcomed birders and tourists alike who would pay the price for their produce, as did Bob Taylor and his friends who "went back to Toronto with the trunk and back of the car filled with delicious apples."[304]

In spite of an obvious interest, and regardless of the fact that they lived in a prime location, few local residents made the study of birds a career. They did, however, take ownership of Point Pelee and got involved in various peripheral organizations such as the Point Pelee Advisory Committee. They became more aware of conservation with the advent of the Nature Reserve. In 1954 the Woodland Nature Trail, which was planned by Stirrett, was built through the Reserve, giving them a place to practice their natural history skills if they wished. Bill Martin describes the original trail:

> It started at what is now called the half-way stop and it sported a small wooden structure as a sort of interpretation spot and a small parking area for about four cars. This is where one picked up checklist cards. This "Stirrett Trail" was the first formal trail but was still only packed earth. When, later, high lake levels raised the water level throughout the park, the trail became boggy and hard to navigate ... Two shelters and seats existed then, one at about post 12 and the other at about post 16 or 17. Unfortunately, these were not cared for or replaced as they deteriorated and have since disappeared. It is hard to describe the Stirrett Trail of those days. It was like entering a medieval cathedral, particularly at the north and south ends.[305]

Wilf Botham was one local naturalist who now had a place to study plants as well as birds but, as Bill Martin points out, in 1956 local naturalists were still outnumbered by the local people who came to Point Pelee for reasons other than the study of nature: "On Victoria Day long weekend ... the park was filled with folk and families from Leamington, laced with a strong contingent of motorcycle gangs and hot-rodders."[306]

One day in 1955, Wilf Botham and a Wheatley area resident, Norm Chesterfield, saw a Yellow-rumped Warbler. Botham let Chesterfield borrow his binoculars and a birder was born. By 1983, Chesterfield had accumulated a life list

Norman Chesterfield, Wheatley area birder in the Guinness Book of World Records.

of 5,556 species of birds, earning him a place in the *Guinness Book of World Records*. His accomplishments were honoured at Point Pelee on April 20, 1988. Norm Chesterfield Day ceremonies took place and activities were run by Park staff. Norm Chesterfield Day is still celebrated every May at Wheatley Provincial Park.

Botham and Chesterfield were not the only birders in Essex County, and by 1964 it was obvious to Tony Pierce, superintendent of Point Pelee National Park, that it was time to start a nature club to bring the growing number of local amateur naturalists together. He, along with Albert D. Law, called a meeting October 27, 1964. James Woodford, managing director of the FON, told the fifty people in attendance that the main purpose of such a club was to develop the interest of adults and youth in natural history and to encourage conservation of natural resources. Mr.

Richard Ussher, vice-president of the FON for southwestern Ontario and park naturalist at Rondeau Provincial Park, also spoke at the meeting, telling those in attendance that Essex County was fortunate to have a national park and a superintendent who was interested in natural history. Wilf Botham described his involvement:

> This evening at 6:30 Ed Keith drove in, wanting to know if I would care to accompany them to Point Pelee, where eight of them were to make plans for a bird club. ... The other six were Dorothy Davie, Tony Pierce, Caroline Simpson, Franklin Anders, Stafford O. Kratz, Al Law. The meeting lasted 3 hours and much was chewed over. A suggested name for the club was Sun Parlour Nature Club.[307]

Ed Keith of Windsor (president), Al Warrick (vice-president), and Stella Pierce (secretary) became the new executive. By the end of January the Sun Parlour Nature Club, which became an affiliate of FON, had eighty-four adult members and twenty juniors. It was a great beginning and was heartily supported by Point Pelee staff.

Their first annual general meeting, in May 1965, started with a picnic at Pete Sikkema's refreshment booth at the Tip. Sikkema was a member of the Club and no doubt offered a reduced price on hamburgers that evening. This would be the location for the Club's annual meeting until Sikkema's decision in 1971 to notify the Canadian government that, because of rowdy youths, he would no longer run the food stand. Sikkema made a contribution not only to the Sun Parlour Nature Club but also to the visiting birders who, even today, remember the food, conversations, and variety of birds seen while resting and eating there. Bill Martin recalls: "The concession stand at the east side of the tip was in full swing and we were able to arrive at the tip area in the morning, order bacon and eggs, toast and coffee, take off and bird in the concession loop and come back in ten minutes to the most welcome dish of sinful food, fighting off the Grackles who were always after our toast. The only other hazard was the omnipresence of Barn Swallows, trying to nest in every crevice of the building."[308]

The Sun Parlour Nature Club lobbied local governments to set up a conservation authority to serve Essex County and Pelee Island. Their concern was the protection of such areas as Hillman Marsh, and in a letter sent March 10, 1972, to the Department of Lands and Forest Fish and Wildlife Division, they asked that Hillman Marsh be bought by the province in order that it be preserved. Happily, Hillman Marsh is now the responsibility of the Essex Region Conservation Authority and continues to be a favourite location for watching birds.

Sun Parlour Nature Club member Wilf Botham died in a car accident in 1989. A year later he was honoured by The Friends of Point Pelee and Point Pelee National Park through the dedication of the Botham Tree Trail in his memory. Many people knew and admired Botham for his broad knowledge, gained through years of self-education. Michael D. Fitzpatrick, a birder and biology teacher from Michigan, recalled an impromptu botany lesson given to him and his wife Sue by Botham:

> One of the most knowledgeable naturalists I've ever met was Wilf Botham. He picked a

leaf off a plant, crumbled it in his hand, and
offered it to Sue and me to smell. I was
delighted by the smell of garlic, one of my
favourite spices. He, however, was appalled by
the plant's presence. He said he had warned
park personnel of its tenacity and pervasive-
ness. Those of us who used to marvel at the
wildflower show that was part of Point Pelee's
allure, now grimace at the sight of this ubiq-
uitous alien, garlic mustard. [309]

By the 1980s, birders and naturalists had other organizations such as the Ontario Field Ornithologists and The
Friends of Point Pelee to join. In consequence, the Sun
Parlour Nature Club, after struggling to survive for a
number of years, handed in its charter.

The Friends of Point Pelee was established in 1981 through
a federal government grant for the formation of co-operating
organizations. The Friends work with the Park without actually being in the Park system. They can recruit volunteers and
offer extra services. Since they are a not-for-profit organization, the Friends can apply for government and other grants,
which the Park cannot do, thus helping out financially as well
as physically. In October 1982, the Friends held an
"Octobirdfest," a one-day event that is held in many locations
across North America. It was only held that one year at Point
Pelee, but it was a tentative first step on the part of the Friends,
under Terry Pratt, their first executive director, toward recognizing the importance of the birders to Point Pelee. Léa
Martell, from Cornwall, was already working for Point Pelee
National Park in 1984 when The Friends of Point Pelee
advertised for a new general manager. She applied and got the

Susan Ross, a Friends of Point Pelee Board member, volunteers her time to serve the Birder's Breakfasts.

job. With seed money acquired through government grants, she set up the Nature Nook Bookstore. Then she forged ahead, hiring staff, encouraging volunteers and helping the Park find funds for various projects.

Martell, along with Point Pelee National Park administrators, who by the mid-1980s were looking for increased funding, set out to see what they could raise from the birders, their single largest user group. One such project was the Festival of Birds, which was kicked off in 1987 and has become an annual event. Park management sent out letters to various companies looking for sponsorship, with the result that Quest Nature Tours and Bushnell Optics became involved. The Festival has evolved over the years to include hikes, special presentations, trips outside of Point Pelee led by Quest, and a binocular clinic run by Bushnell. Quest and Bushnell provide some of the prizes for an annual raffle, the "Keep the Songs Alive" sweepstakes. The sale of tickets for the wonderful prizes made this an excellent Park fundraiser. Their combined efforts, with the support of birders, has helped to raise a considerable amount of money over the years.

Martell stayed on as general manager for the Friends until November 2002. By the time she left, the Nature

Nook Bookstore at the Visitor Centre, the Cattail Café at the Marsh Boardwalk, and the shuttle system, run "at cost" by the Friends, were all part of a growing list of support services provided by The Friends of Point Pelee to Point Pelee National Park and its visitors.

Under the management of Martell, the Friends also published several Pelee-specific bird books. *Warblers of Point Pelee* and *Sparrows of Point Pelee* are still sold at the Nature Nook Bookstore. This little shop provides other up-to-date nature books as well as the usual knick-knacks and souvenirs. Many birders, including those who are not local, carry membership cards to The Friends of Point Pelee that allow them a ten per cent discount on their purchases.

Another popular service delivered directly to the birders from The Friends of Point Pelee is the Birder's Breakfast and Lunch, which is set up behind the Visitor Centre. With the loss of the Tip concession stand to erosion in the late 1980s, this has become almost a necessity, as the only other place left where food can be obtained within the confines of the Park is at the Marsh Boardwalk. With parking around the Visitor Centre at a premium on May mornings, many birders are reluctant to move their cars and would be forced to go without breakfast, whereas a coffee and bagel, muffin, or doughnut will hold them over until they are ready to move northward within the Park in search of birds. Under the circumstances, feeding the birders keeps The Friends volunteers hopping. May has become the busiest single month of the season for The Friends and they, in turn, have worked to cater to the needs of the birdwatching public. It has been of mutual benefit. If the birders are sometimes irritated by Park rules, that feeling is offset by the hospitality shown them by the Friends. The Certificate of Appreciation

The Pelee shuttle pulls into the Tip Circle.

given to Léa and the Friends of Point Pelee by the Ontario Field Ornithologists in 1999 could be taken as a thank you to all those local residents who have ever gone out of their way to make birders feel welcome to Point Pelee and the surrounding area.

As for the birders, without question they have arrived. From haphazard to organized, from being ignored to being wooed, the birders of Point Pelee National Park have risen out of obscurity into the limelight.

Notes

Chapter 1

[1] W. H. Ballou, "Birds and Wild Rice," *Oologist* 3 (1877): 57.

[2] Lieut. Col. C. B. Comstock, Corps of Engineers, Brevet Brigadier-General, U. S. A, Aided by the assistants on the Survey, *Report Upon The Primary Triangulation of the United States Lake Survey* (Washington, Government Printing Office 1882): 38-39.

[3] 45th Congress 2nd Session House of Representatives, *Annual Report of the Chief of Engineers to the Secretary of War for the Year 1877*. Part I (Washington, Government Printing Office 1877): Appendix II.

[4] W. H Ballou, "The Natural History of the Islands of Lake Erie," *Field and Forest* 3 (1878): 135-137.

[5] Ballou, "Ornithological Notes," *Oologist* 3 (1877): 57.

[6] The N. A. Marquis Company, *Who Was Who In America: A Companion Biographical Reference Work to Who's Who in America* 2 (Chicago Il. USA 1950): 41-42.

[7] Dr. William Brodie, letter to Percy A. Taverner, Great Lakes Ornithological Club documents, Royal Ontario Museum, Toronto.

[8] Dr. William Brodie, letter to Taverner.

[9] Shannon Michael Quinn, "The Natural History of a Collector: J. H. Fleming (1872-1940)," diss., Graduate Program of Environmental Studies, York University, 1995: 111.

Chapter 2

[10] Harry Gould, "Bird Notes From Point Pelee, Ontario," *Ontario Naturalist* 15 (1901): 15-16.

[11] W.E. Saunders, "The Black-throated Bunting, Yellow-breasted Chat, and Connecticut Warbler in Ontario" *The Auk* 2 (1885): 307–308.

[12] Percy A. Taverner, Bradshaw Hall Swales, "The Birds of Point Pelee," *The Wilson Bulletin* 19 (1907): 49-50.

[13] Taverner, Swales, "The Birds," 19: 90.

[14] Taverner, Swales, "The Birds," 19: 135.

[15] John L. Cranmer-Byng, "A Life With Birds: Percy A. Taverner, Canadian Ornithologist, 1875-1947," *Canadian Field Naturalist* 110 (The Ottawa Field Naturalists' Club, Ottawa 1996): 23.

[16] Cranmer-Byng, "A Life With Birds": 24.

[17] Cranmer-Byng, "A Life With Birds": 24.

[18] Cranmer-Byng, "A Life With Birds": 24.

[19] Cranmer-Byng, "A Life With Birds": 24.

[20] Marianne Gosztonyi Ainley, "The Contribution of the Amateur to North American Ornithology: A Historical Perspective," diss., Institute D'Histoire et de Sociopolitique Des Sciences, Universite De Montreal, Montreal, Quebec: 167.

[21] Lynds Jones, "The Birds of Cedar Point and Vicinity," *The Wilson Bulletin* 21 (1909): 65.

[22] Taverner and Swales, "The Birds," 19: 46.

[23] Percy A. Taverner, notes 15 Sept. 1906, GLOC documents, Royal Ontario

Museum, Toronto.

[24] P.A. Taverner, GLOC papers, Royal Ontario Museum.

[25] W.E. Saunders, "Summer Birds of the Southern Edge of Western Ontario," *The Wilson Bulletin* 21 (1909): 152-155.

[26] W.E. Saunders, "Summer Birds": 152.

[27] W.E. Saunders, "Tufted Tit – A New Record for Canada," *The Auk* 31 (1914): 402.

[28] W.E. Saunders, "The Status of the Bewick's Wren in Ontario," *The Canadian Field-Naturalist* 33 (1919): 118.

[29] W.E. Saunders, "Bachman's Sparrow An Addition to the Canadian Fauna," *The Canadian Field-Naturalist* 33 (1919): 118.

[30] W.E. Saunders, "New Records for Point Pelee," *The Canadian Field-Naturalist* 38 (1924): 37.

[31] Taverner, GLOC documents, Royal Ontario Museum.

[32] Taverner, Swales "The Birds of Point Pelee," *The Wilson Bulletin* 20 (1908): 118.

[33] Taverner, Swales, "The Birds," 20:119-120.

[34] W.E. Saunders, "Summer Tanager," *The Auk* 26 (1909).

[35] W.E. Saunders, "Point Pelee May 8-11, 1909," Saunders papers, Royal Ontario Museum.

[36] Taverner, GLOC documents, Royal Ontario Museum.

Chapter 3

[37] Charles W. Richmond, "Bradshaw Hall Swales, 1875-1928," *The Auk* 45 (1928):321-324.

[38] Cranmer-Byng, "A Life With Birds": 19.

[39] Cranmer-Byng, "A Life With Birds": 22.

[40] Cranmer-Byng, "A Life With Birds": 22.

[41] Cranmer-Byng, "The Great Lakes Ornithological Club The Origin and Early Years, 1905-1911," *Ontario Birds* 2 (1984): 6.

[42] Cranmer-Byng, "The Great Lakes Ornithological Club": 9.

[43] John Cranmer-Byng, "The Bulletin of the Great Lakes Ornithological Club, 1905-1909," *Ontario Birds* 3 (1985): 49.

[44] Dr. William Brodie, letter to Taverner, GLOC documents, ROM.

[45] Cranmer-Byng, "A Life With Birds": 34.

[46] Cranmer-Byng, "A Life With Birds": 34.

[47] Cranmer-Byng, "The Great Lakes Ornithological Club": 5-6.

[48] Taverner and Swales, "The Birds of Point Pelee," *The Wilson Bulletin* 19 (1907): 37-38.

[49] Taverner and Swales, "The Birds," 19: 38-45.

[50] Taverner and Swales, "The Birds," 19: 45.

[51] Taverner and Swales, "The Birds," 19: 46.

[52] Taverner and Swales, "The Birds," *The Wilson Bulletin* 20 (1908): 129.

[53] P.A. Taverner, letter to Fleming GLOC papers, ROM.

[54] P. A. Taverner, letter to Fleming GLOC papers, ROM.

[55] P. A. Taverner, "Memories of William Edwin Saunders," *The Auk* 61, (1944): 349.

[56] Richmond, "Bradshaw Hall Swales": 321-324.

[57] Cranmer-Byng, "The Great Lakes": 4 – 12.

[58] W.E. Saunders, "In memoriam James Stirton Wallace," *The Canadian Field-Naturalist* 37 (1923): 74-75.

[59] W.E. Saunders, GLOC documents, ROM.

[60] W.E. Saunders, GLOC documents, ROM.

[61] P. A. Taverner, "Memories of William Edwin Saunders": 350.

[62] Martin K. McNicholl, John L. Cranmer-Byng, *Ornithology in Ontario* (Burlington: Ontario Field Ornithologists, Hawk Owl Publishing, 1994): 347.

[63] Charles Maddeford, letter to Alan Wormington, May 22, 1982.

[64] W.E. Saunders, "A Grandstand Seat at Point Pelee," *London Free Press* 3 Oct. 1931.

[65] W.W. Judd, *Early Naturalists and Natural History Societies of London, Ontario* (London ON: Phelps, 1979): 22-58.

[66] McNicholl, Cranmer-Byng, *Ornithology in Ontario*: 192.

[67] W.E. Saunders, "Nature Week by Week; Federation of Ontario naturalists," *London Free Press* 5 March 1932.

[68] Kent Nature Club, "Federation of Ontario Naturalists - Regional Gathering," Program.

[69] McNicholl, Cranmer-Byng, *Ornithology*: 209.

[70] McNicholl, Cranmer-Byng, *Ornithology*: 211.

[71] James L. Baillie, "Highlights of Point Pelee," presentation to Toronto Ornithological Club, 9 June 1969. Thomas Fisher Rare Book Museum Box 40: 5.

[72] Baillie, "Highlights," presentation 1969.

[73] Harold Lancaster, email to author, 4 Jan. 2003.

[74] William A. Martin, "Point Pelee Memories: 1956 to 1999," *Point Pelee Natural History* News 3 (2003):37-41.

[75] Shannon Michael Quinn, "The Natural History of a Collector: J.H. Fleming(1872-1940)" diss., York University, 1995, 273-275.

[76] Quinn, "The Natural History": 240-241.

[77] McNicholl, Cranmer-Byng, *Ornithology*: 172.

[78] McNicholl, Cranmer-Byng, *Ornithology*: 175.

[79] Cranmer-Byng, "A Life With Birds": 42 - 49.

[80] P.A. Taverner, "Some Raptorial Migrations in Southern Ontario," *Ottawa Naturalist* 25 (1911): 77.

[81] Quinn, "The Natural History": 243.

[82] W.W. Judd, *More Naturalists and Their Work in Southern Ontario* (London Ontario: The Hern/Kelly Printing Company Limited 1992): 30-31.

[83] Richmond, "Bradshaw": 321-324.

[84] N.A. Wood, "Bird Migration at Point Pelee" *The Wilson Bulletin* 22 (1910): 63-78.

[85] Donald Bucknell, letter to author, 7 Dec. 2003.

Chapter 4

[86] Michael Shannon Quinn, "The Natural History of a Collector: J. H. Fleming," diss., York University, (1995): 126.

[87] Quinn, "The Natural History of a Collector": 265.

[88] Geological and National History Survey of Canada Reports of Explorations and Surveys 1880-81-82 Geological Survey of Canada Operations of the

Geological Corps.: 25-25

[89] William Saunders, "Brief Notes Of A Trip To Point Pelee, With Additions To Our List Of Canadian Butterflies," *Canadian Entomologist* 16 (1885): 50-53

[90] W.A. Waiser, *The Field Naturalist John Macoun*, The Geological Survey, and Natural Science (Toronto: University of Toronto Press 1989): 76

[91] Geological Survey Department, "GSC Annual Report" 14 (1901): 154A.

[92] Michael Quinn, *The Natural History of a Collector*: 71.

[93] Cranmer-Byng, "A Life With Birds": 25.

[94] Taverner, GLOC documents, ROM.

[95] Janet Foster, *Working For Wildlife* (Toronto: University of Toronto Press 1978): 125.

[96] Quinn, "The Natural History": 168-169.

[97] Taverner, GLOC documents, ROM.

[98] Taverner, GLOC documents, ROM.

[99] Taverner, GLOC documents, ROM.

[100] Taverner, Swales, "The Birds," *The Wilson Bulletin* 20 (1908): 81.

[101] W. E. Saunders, "The Mockingbird in Ontario," *The Canadian Field-Naturalist* 37 (1923): 116-117.

[102] Taverner, Swales, "The Birds," 19: 146.

[103] Cranmer-Byng, "A Life With Birds": 43.

[104] P.A. Taverner, "Geological Survey Museum Work on Point Pelee Ont.," *The Ottawa Naturalist* 28 (1914): 105.

[105] W.E. Saunders, letter to Swales, 29 June 1913, GLOC documents, ROM.

[106] P. A. Taverner, "Geological Survey Museum Work on Point Pelee Ont.," *Ottawa Naturalist* 28 (1914): 105.

[107] Joseph Kastner, *A World of Watchers* (New York: Alfred A. Knopf 1986).

[108] Elliot Coues, *Field Ornithology, Comprising a Manual of Instruction for Procuring Preparing and Preserving Birds and a Check-list of North American Birds* (Salem Naturalists' Agency, 1874): 5.

[109] William Wyett, "First Ontario Specimen of Mountain Bluebird Collected at Point Pelee," *Ontario Field Biologist* 20 (1966): 42.

[110] William Wyett, "First Canadian Specimen of Bell's Vireo," *The Canadian Field-Naturalist* 85 (1971): 327-328 (CNM 57428).

[111] Lester L. Snyder, "Collecting Birds and Conservation," *Ontario Field Biologist* 12 (1958): 16-17.

Chapter 5

[112] James Woodford, "The Use of Mist Nets and a Heligoland Trap at Point Pelee," *Bird Banding* 30 (1959): 38-45.

[113] Hoyes Lloyd, "Point Pelee Should Have a Bird Banding Station," *The Canadian Field-Naturalist* 41 (1927): 89.

[114] George M. Stirrett, P*oint Pelee, Ontario: A Migratory Pathway for Birds and Insects* (Ottawa: National and Historic Parks Branch Department of Indian Affairs and Northern Development, 1970): 91.

[115] Stirrett, *Point Pelee, Ontario: A Migratory Pathway*: 91.

[116] James L. Baillie, "Highlights of Point Pelee."

[117] Don MacDonald, "Pelee Notes," a personal, unpublished journal (1940-1948).

[118] William W. H. Gunn, "Reverse Migration in the Pelee Region in Relation to the Weather," diss., University of Toronto School of Graduate Studies, 1951.

[119] William W. H. Gunn, "A Banding Station at Point Pelee," *FON Bulletin* 64 (1954): 25.

[120] James Woodford, interview with the author, 1999.

[121] James Woodford, "Point Pelee Banding Station – Spring, 1956," *Ontario Bird Banders' Association Banding Newsletter* 4 (1957): 4.

[122] William A. Martin, "Point Pelee Memories 1956 to 1999": 37-41.

[123] Robert R. Taylor, "Robert R. Taylor & Point Pelee," unpublished manuscript, 3 May 2002.

[124] Stirrett, Point Pelee, Ontario, *A Migratory Pathway*: 15.

[125] Master Plan Point Pelee National Park (Parks Canada 1972): 17.

[126] William A. Martin, "Point Pelee Memories 1956 to 1999": 37-41

[127] "Point Pelee," Ontario Bird Banding Association October 1960.

[128] "Point Pelee," Ontario Bird Banding Association September 1961.

[129] J.O.L. Roberts, "Point Pelee Banding Station Report for Years 1959 Through 1962," *Ontario Bird Banding* 2 (1966): 1-28.

[130] Jane Evans, bird banding notes, 29 September 1973.

[131] Dennis Rupert, "Point Pelee Bird Observatory 1973 Report."

[132] Ross Snider, bird banding notes, 16 October, 1973.

[133] Bill Wasserfall, bird banding notes, 29 October 1973.

[134] Marianne Gosztonyi Ainley, "The Contribution of the Amateur to North American Ornithology: A Historical Perspective," diss., Institut D'Histoire Et De Sociopolitique Des Sciences Universite De Montreal, Montreal, Quebec, Canada: 169.

Chapter 6

[135] Richard M. Saunders, Flashing Wings (Toronto: McClelland and Stewart 1947): 147.

[136] Joseph Kastner, *A World of Watchers* (New York: Alfred A. Knopf 1986).

[137] Percy A. Taverner, letter to Fleming 16 June 1909, GLOC documents ROM.

[138] James H. Fleming, letter to Taverner 26 Sept 1907, GLOC documents ROM.

[139] Quinn, "The Natural History": 101.

[140] Quinn, "The Natural History": 248-249.

[141] Ron Tasker, "J. Bruce Falls: Distinguished Ornithologist," *Ontario Birds* 20 (2002): 144 -149.

[142] Fred Bodsworth, "Beginnings," *Toronto Field Naturalist* 399 (1988): 6-7.

[143] Barb and Don Cavin, interview with Robert R. Taylor, 1999.

[144] Jean Kelly, "Birding at Pelee," letter to the author, 6 Jan. 2004.

[145] Kevin Mclaughlin, letter to author, 2002.

[146] Joseph Kastner, *A World of Watchers*.

[147] McNicholl, Cranmer-Byng, *Ornithology*: 84.

[148] Tom Hince, interview with author 2003.

[149] W. W. H. Gunn, "Work in Progress on 'Sounds of Nature'," *FON Bulletin* 87 (1960): 35-36.

[150] Donald R. Gunn, "Records for Naturalists," *FON Bulletin* 88 (1960): 38-39.

[151] Don MacDonald, "Pelee Notes," a personal journal.

[152] Ron Tasker, "J. Bruce Falls," *Ontario Birds* 20 (2002): 145.

[153] Bristol Foster, interview with Robert R. Taylor 1999.

[154] Fred Bodsworth, interview with author November 2000.

[155] Robert Curry, email, 21 Jan. 2000.

[156] Peter A. Coe, interview with author, May 2003.

[157] Don MacDonald, "Pelee Notes."

[158] James Woodford, interview with author, 1999.

[159] Robert R. Taylor, "Point Pelee Memories," unpublished manuscript.

[160] Curry, email to author, 2000.

[161] Alan Wormington, "Introduction," *Point Pelee* by William Reynolds (Toronto: Oxford University Press 1981): 5-6.

[162] Kevin McLaughlin, letter to author, 2002.

[163] Barry Griffiths, interview with Robert R. Taylor, 1999.

[164] Jim Coey, email, 23 Jan. 2000.

[165] Richard M. Saunders, *Flashing Wings*: 144-145.

[166] Don and Barb Cavin, interview with Robert R. Taylor, 1999.

[167] Robert R. Taylor , "Robert R. Taylor & Point Pelee."

[168] Robert R. Taylor, "Robert R. Taylor & Point Pelee".

[169] William Martin, "Point Pelee Memories 1956 to 1999": 37-41.

[170] Tom Hince, interview with author, 2003.

[171] Alan Wormington, "White-faced Ibis: New to Point Pelee" *Point Pelee Natural History News* 3 (2003): 21-22

[172] Quinn, "The Natural History": 61.

[173] Peter Whalen, "Point Pelee's late-May show tops," *Globe and Mail* 30 May 1987.

[174] A. Wormington, "A History of Numbers" email to author March 2006.

[175] Fred Bodsworth, "Beginnings": 7.

Chapter 7

[176] Alan L. Contreras, "The Past Present and Future of Field Ornithology," *North American Birds* 45 (2000): 345-347.

[177] M. T. Myres, "Science and Sight-Records," *Ontario Naturalist* 1 (1963): 16 – 20.

[178] Robert Curry, "In Memoriam: George Webster North (1910 - 1983)," *Ontario Birds* 2 (1984): 3.

[179] John MacArthur, "Early Days at Point Pelee," email to author, 23 May 2003.

[180] Gerry Bennett, personal journal.

[181] Robert Curry, "Chuck-wills-widow: Second Record for Point Pelee, Third for Ontario," *Point Pelee Natural History News* 2 (2002): 28.

[182] Robert Curry, email, 2000.

[183] Gosztonyi, "The Contribution": 168.

[184] Alan Wormington, "The Point Pelee Lesser Nighthawk: A Unique Record for Ontario and Canada," *Point Pelee Natural History News* 2 (2002): 1.

[185] W. Earl Godfrey, letter to Alan Wormington, dated 31 May 1974.

[186] Clive Goodwin, letter to R. A. Watt, Chief Park Naturalist, Point Pelee National Park, 11 August, 1980.

[187] Mark Cocker, *Birders: Tales of a Tribe* (New York, NY: Atlantic Monthly

Press 2001): 86.

188 M. T. Myres, *The Ontario Naturalist* 1 (1963): 20.
189 Clive Goodwin, "Birds, Birdwatching and Record-keeping," *FON Bulletin* 8 (1970): 13-15.
190 Kim Eckert, "The 1980 Big Day Report," *Birding* 13 (1981): 22-24.
191 Daniel F. Brunton, Letter to R. Arbib Editor of American Birds, 19 October, 1981.
192 Ross D. James, "Ontario Bird Records Committee Report for 1982," *Ontario Birds* 1 (1983): 7.
193 Ron Ridout, "From the President," *Ontario Birds* 1 (1983): 2.
194 James M. Richards, "Once upon a time," *Ontario Birds* 1 (1983): 6.
195 Clive Goodwin, interview with author, 24 June 2006.
196 Ron D. Weir, "Information Wanted," *Ontario Birds* 1 (1983): 73-75.
197 "OFO Announcements," *Ontario Birds* 2 (1984): 52.
198 Alan Wormington, Ross D. James, "Ontario Bird Records Committee, Checklist of the Birds of Ontario," *Ontario Birds* 2 (1984): 13.
199 Peter Whalen, "Daredevil Whimbrel return for annual air show," *Globe and Mail* 29 May 1985.
200 Peter Whalen, "Patient Birders Hit the Jackpot," *Globe and Mail* 20 May 1989.
201 "A Proud Record" *Ontario Birding* 2: 3 (1997): 12
202 Don Lajoie, "Birders Want a Rematch," *Windsor Star,* 2001.
203 Hince Tom, email to author, 22 June, 2006.
204 Sharon Oosthoek, "The Bird That Got Away," *Seasons* 42 (2002): 15-17.
205 Alan Wormington, "Point Pelee 2005—A Big Year Like No Other," *OFO News* 24 (2006): 1-5.

Chapter 8

206 Gerry Shemilt, interview with author 25 Nov. 2003.
207 Janet Foster, *Working For Wildlife* (Toronto: University of Toronto Press 1978): 36-38.
208 Janet Foster, *Working For Wildlife*: 158.
209 Environment Canada Press Release, *Minister Orders End To Duck Hunting At Point Pelee National Park*, 6 June 1989.
210 J. R. Dymond, "Conservation Efforts and Accomplishments of the Federation," *FON Bulletin* 71 (1956).
211 Hugh Halliday, Senn, Harrison F. Lewis, *Dominion Parks Bureau Investigation* (Department of Mines and Resources and the Division of Botany, Science Service, Department of Agriculture 1939).
212 W. W. H. Gunn, "Pelee Letter," *FON Bulletin* 61 (1953).
213 R. M. Saunders, *Flashing Wings* (Toronto: McClelland and Stewart Ltd. 1947): 144-146.
214 Don MacDonald, "Birding Notes."
215 J.G. Battin, J.G. Nelson, *Man's Impact on Point Pelee National Park* (Toronto: National and Provincial Parks Association of Canada 1978): 120.
216 Tim Findlay, "5 Years at Point Make Big Change," *Windsor Star* 12 August 1964.
217 William Clark, letter to Robert R. Taylor, 1 June 1999.

[218] John S. Tener, *First Interim Report of the Ecological Study of Point Pelee National Park* (Ottawa, 1949).

[219] Fred Bodsworth, interview with author, November 2000.

[220] Ron Steele, "Summer Will Return Not 'Mr. Pelee' Frith," *Windsor Star* 14 Sept. 1963.

[221] Grant J. Glassco, Eugene F. Therrien, Watson Sellar, *Royal Commission On Government Organization Vol. 2 Supporting Services For Government* (Ottawa: Queen's Printer 1962): 38-39.

[222] Bob Meyer, "$7.5 Million for Point Pelee," *Windsor Star* 1967.

[223] Wilf Botham, letter written to Gerald B. McKeating Executive Director FON, 13 Nov. 1967.

[224] Cordy Tymstra, Russ Dowham, *Resource Management Plan For Birding As A Park Activity At Point Pelee National Park* (Natural Resource Conservation Division Parks Canada Ontario Region 1978): 6.

[225] D. A. Wilkes, comments regarding the *Resource Management Plan For Birding As A Park Activity At Point Pelee National Park* 8 January 1978.

[226] G. Tom Hince, interview with author 2003.

[227] William Clark, letter to Robert R. Taylor, 1 June 1999.

[228] Wilf Botham, *Selections From an Amateur Naturalist's Notes* (1977).

[229] W. W. H. Gunn , "Point Pelee Letter - Spring, 1955," *FON Bulletin* 69 (1955): 26-28.

[230] William Clark, letter to Robert R. Taylor, 1 June 1999.

[231] William Martin, letter to superintendent Point Pelee National Park, 28 January 1992.

[232] Robert R. Taylor, email to author, 25 May 2002.

[233] Robert Sachs, email 15 Feb. 2000.

[234] Wilf Botham, *Selections From an Amateur Naturalist's Notes* (1977)

[235] Tom Hince, email to author, 13 June 2002.

[236] Fred Bodsworth, "Bodsworth" *The Pierre Berton Celebration Dinner* Toronto, Royal York Hotel, 28 Feb. 1979.

[237] Dr. James R. Butler, Gregory D. Fenton M.Sc., *Bird Watchers of Point Pelee National Park, Ontario: Their Characteristics and Activities, With Special Consideration to Their Social and Resource Impacts,* (Edmonton: Wildland Recreation Program Department of Forest Science the University of Alberta 1988): 65.

[238] Bill Clark, letter to Robert R. Taylor, 1 June 1999.

[239] Botham, *Selections From an Amateur Naturalist's Notes.*

[240] George Stirrett, *Point Pelee National Park A Migration Highway* (Ottawa: National and Historic Parks Branch Department of Indian Affairs and Northern Development, 1970): 82.

[241] William A. Martin, letter to superintendent of Point Pelee National Park, 28 January 1992.

[242] Alan Wormington, letter to members of Point Pelee Natural History Research Committee, 2002.

[243] Panel on Ecological Integrity of Canada's National Parks, *Unimpaired for Future Generations Vol. II: Setting a New Direction for Canada's National Parks* (Ottawa: Minister of Public Works and Government Services 2000): 10-3.

[244] North-South Environmental Inc., *State of the Park Report Point Pelee National Park* (Campbellville, Ontario, October, 2000):6 -23.
[245] *Unimpaired*: 2-16, 2-17.
[246] Kelly Hulme, email, 22 Jan. 2000.
[247] John C. Devlin, Grace Naismith, *The World of Roger Tory Peterson* (Montreal: Optimum Publishing Company 1977): 74.
[248] Sandra Eadie, "The Importance of Nature," *OFO News* 17:3 (1999): 11.

Chapter 9
[249] William Gunn, "Pelee Letter," *FON Bulletin* 61 (May 1953): 9.
[250] Hugh M. Halliday, "If You Want to See Birds," *Star Weekly* 16 Oct. 1954.
[251] Peter Whalen, "Point Pelee, Ont.," *Globe and Mail* 20 May 1987.
[252] Peter Whalen, "A rainbow of Migrants invades Point Pelee," *Globe and Mail* 14 May 1988.
[253] Glen Hvenegaard, Doug Krystofiak, "Birdwatchers of Point Pelee, A Socio-Economic Impact Assessment Concerning Birders and the Point Pelee-Leamington District," diss., University of Alberta, 1987: 67.
[254] Peter Alan Coe, interview with author, May 2003.
[255] Joanie Piluke, interview with author, 2003.
[256] Ron Austing, with Robert R. Taylor, May 1999.
[257] Keith Reynolds, "The Fall at Point Pelee," *London Free Press* 22 Oct. 1949.
[258] Botham, *Selections From an Amateur Naturalist's Notes*
[259] Rowley Frith, "Point Pelee National Park," *The Ontario Naturalist* 2 (1964): 11 – 17.
[260] Tom Hayman, "Several Waves of wood warblers seen as warm air moves into southern Ontario," *London Free Press* 22 May 1975.
[261] Peter Whalen, *Globe and Mail* 12 May 1982.
[262] Jack McKenzie, "Here's Why Birders Watch" *Globe and Mail* 4 May 1968.
[263] Glen Hvenegaard, Doug Krystofiak, "Birdwatchers of Point Pelee": 50, 73, 88.
[264] Sigrid McFarlan, interview with Robert R. Taylor, 1999.
[265] Glen Hvenegaard, Doug Krystofiak, "Birdwatchers of Point Pelee": 65.
[266] Peter A. Coe, interview with author, May 2003.
[267] "1999 ABA Membership Survey," conducted by Surveys and Strategies.
[268] Turcotte Patrice, "Vingt-cinq année d'observations printanieres qu parc national de la Pointe-Pelee," *Le Naturaliste Canadien* hiver 2000/2001.
[269] Carol McNall, "Birding at Pelee," letter to author, Dec. 2003.

Chapter 10
[270] W.E. Saunders, GLOC documents ROM.
[271] Robert Stewart, personal communication, May 2004
[272] W. W. Judd, personal communication, Dec. 2002.
[273] W.E. Saunders, "Evening Grosbeaks," *London Free Press* 11 January 1930.
[274] Keith Reynolds, "Early Birds on Pelee," *London Free Press* 22 April 1950.
[275] Keith Reynolds, "Pelee weekend 1950," *London Free Press* 20 May 1950.
[276] Tom Hayman, "Northern Three-Toed Woodpecker spotted at Point Pelee," *London Free Press* 9 Jan. 1975.
[277] L. Anglin, "Birder Extraordinaire—The Life and Legacy of James L. Baillie (1904-1970)," (Toronto: Ornithological Club and Long Point Bird

Observatory 1992).

[278] James Baillie, "Wildlife, European Duck Seen in Ontario," *The Toronto Telegram* May 1965.

[279] Gordon Bellerby, personal interview, 1999.

[280] Peter Whalen, "Early birders miss a prize sighting," *Globe and Mail* 27 May 1989.

[281] "Naturalists to Stage Point Pelee Outing," *Leamington Post* 29 April 1965.

[282] "Hunters and Naturalists Bird boom at Point Pelee," *Windsor Star* 2 Oct. 1972.

[283] O. S. Pettingill, "Bird Finding: Spring Migration at Point Pelee," *Audubon* (March-April 1964): 78-80.

[284] George H. Harrison, *Roger Tory Peterson's Dozen Birding Hotspots* (New York, Simon and Schuster, 1976): 105.

[285] John Allen Livingston, "At Point Pelee In The Spring," *The Bird Watcher's America* edited by Olin Sewall Pettingill Jr., (New York: Laboratory of Ornithology, Cornell University, McGraw-Hill Book Company 1965): 347-355.

[286] Clive E. Goodwin, *A Bird-finding Guide to Ontario* (Toronto: University of Toronto Press 1982): 51.

[287] Clive E. Goodwin, *The Traveling Birder* (New York: Doubleday 1991): 50-64.

[288] William J. Crins, "Point Pelee National Park," *A Bird-Finding Guide to Canada* edited by J. C. Finlay (Edmonton: Hurtig Publishers Ltd. 1984): 177-180.

[289] Tom Hince, *A Birder's Guide to Point Pelee* (Windsor ON: Tom Hince): 48.

[290] Pete Dunne, Linda Dunne, *The Feather Quest* (New York: Dutton, Penguin Books 1992): 105-106.

[291] Gerry Bennett, *Wild Birdwatchers I Have Known* (G. Bennett, Webcom Limited 1977).

[292] Gerry Bennett, "Statisticae Canadensis," *Birdfinding in Canada* 4 (1982): 9-11.

[293] Gerry Bennett, "Pilgrimage to Point Pelee - Part Five," *Birdfinding in Canada* 4.3 (1984): 1.

[294] Murray J. Speirs, "Worth Noting," *FON Bulletin* 82 (1958): 32.

[295] Alan Wormington, "Noteworthy Bird Records," *Point Pelee Natural History News* (2001 - 2003).

[296] W. W. H. Gunn, "Point Pelee, May 10, 1952," *F O N Bulletin* 57 (1952).

[297] Tom Hince, interview with author, September 2003.

[298] W. W. H. Gunn , "Pelee Letter, May, 1954," *FON Bulletin* 65 (1954): 34-38.

[299] Tom Hince, *A Birder's Guide*: 127.

[300] Dave Milsom, email 28 Jan. 2000.

[301] "Certificates of Appreciation 1999," *OFO News* 18.1 (2000): 11.

[302] Reynolds Keith, "More Hawk Migration," *London Free Press* 4 Oct. 1947.

[303] Robert Sachs, email, 4 Feb. 2000.

[304] Robert R. Taylor, "Robert R. Taylor & Point Pelee," 3 May 2002.

[305] William A. Martin, "Point Pelee Memories: 1956 – 1999," *Point Pelee Natural History News* 3 (2003): 37-41.

[306] Martin, "Point Pelee Memories": 37-41.

[307] Wilf Botham, *Selections From an Amateur Naturalist's Notes*

[308] Martin, "Point Pelee Memories": 37-41.

[309] Michael Fitzpatrick, personal notes, 13 Nov. 2003.